HOW TO HAVE A
GREAT
LIFE

35 SURPRISINGLY
SIMPLE WAYS TO
SUCCESS

FULFILLMENT & HAPPINESS

PAUL McGEE

CAPSTONE
A Wiley Brand

Registered office
John Wiley & Sons Ltd, The Atrium, Southern Gate, Chichester, West Sussex, PO19 8SQ, United Kingdom

For details of our global editorial offices, for customer services and for information about how to apply for permission to reuse the copyright material in this book please see our website at www.wiley.com.

Library of Congress Cataloging-in-Publication Data

Names: McGee, Paul, 1964- author.
Title: How to have a great life : 35 surprisingly simple ways to success, fulfilment and happiness / by Paul McGee.
Description: First edition. | Southern Gate, Chichester, West Sussex : Wiley, 2018. |
Identifiers: LCCN 2018008700 (print) | ISBN 9780857087751 (pbk.)
Subjects: LCSH: Self-actualization (Psychology) | Success. | Self-realization. | Happiness.
Classification: LCC BF637.S4 .M239 2018 (print) | DDC 158–dc23
LC record available at https://lccn.loc.gov/2018008700

A catalogue record for this book is available from the British Library.
ISBN 978–0–857–08775–1 (pbk) ISBN 978–0–857–08778–2 (ebk)
ISBN 978–0–857–08777–5 (ebk)

10 9 8 7 6 5 4 3 2 1

Cover Design: Wiley

Set in 11/15 pt NewBaskervilleStd-Roman by Thomson Digital, Noida, India

Printed in Great Britain by TJ International Ltd, Padstow, Cornwall, UK

To Matt and Ruffio

with love

Contents

Introduction

MAKE SURE YOU READ THIS

The likelihood is that you and I have never met. So, as we embark on what at times will be a deeply personal journey, I wanted to share what's inspired and also shaped and influenced the words you are about to read.

I've been writing books for over 20 years. This is my eleventh and I'm incredibly excited about writing this one, even more so than my previous books. Were I ever to have grandchildren, this would be the first book of mine I'd like them to read. I think it contains some life lessons that I know will be of huge benefit for them to learn.

But I've also struggled in writing this book for one simple reason:

I feel a fraud and a sense of arrogance in doing so.

Why?

Well, I've had to ask myself the question 'Who am I to write a book called *How to Have a Great Life?*' Am I assuming that your life isn't so great, and that I have all the answers? Can I honestly look back on over half a century on this planet and describe my life as great?

To be honest, I cringe at such a thought. Like many people, my life at times has been a rollercoaster. I've certainly enjoyed some highs, but I've also endured some lows.

So, cards on the table. We're embarking on a journey together, and I hope when it ends you feel it's been a worthwhile, enjoyable, and stimulating ride. But we're doing this together. You and me. I'm convinced you'll discover ideas and insights that will enhance your life, and that will bring increased success, fulfilment, and happiness.

But equally, so will I.

We're all on a learning journey together, and the words I write don't come from a place of smug, superior self-satisfaction, but more from a place of surprise that, despite my occasional screw-ups, stumbles, and struggles over the years, I've learnt quite a few things along the way and had some successes too.

I'm genuinely excited by this book because I believe what you're about to read is hugely important. It's about the most crucial topic you'll ever explore – your life and how to make the most of it. The reality is, whatever our age, gender, culture, or background, we all have similar needs. We all want to be loved. To belong. To have a sense of purpose. And perhaps without even realizing it, we spend the whole of our lives trying to meet and fulfil those needs.

The question is, how can you increase your chances of fulfilling those needs and avoid the potential pitfalls, blind alleys, and possibly even roads to self-destruction?

That's what this book is about.

My own life experience has been wide and varied. I've worked in a job I detested, trained as a probation officer, nursed terminally ill cancer patients, and lost a high-flying graduate management role with a global brand through ill-health. I've also managed 30 women on the economy beef burger line at a frozen food company. If you've never managed 30 women you haven't lived. If you've never eaten economy beef burgers, you're lucky.

I've been running my own business for over 26 years. During that time, I've worked with teachers, entrepreneurs, salespeople, nurses, politicians, Premier League footballers, business gurus, and chief executives.

And during that time, I've learnt this: if theories are great, trust me, experience has been priceless.

And it's many of these life experiences that I'll be drawing on in order to help us discover the insights, ideas, and inspiration required to have a great life.

You'll notice I use stories a lot. Stories stick, and their appeal spans all ages and cultures. I'll be sharing my struggles as well as my successes. My brand of motivation is Mancunian in nature (I was born in South Manchester), rather than Californian. Less ra ra, more reality.

I'm also conscious that, despite many people's desire to develop and improve their lives, they increasingly seem to have less and less time to do so. I'm a huge fan of personal development books, but even I feel somewhat daunted at the prospect of wading through hundreds of pages of small typeface in search of my latest insight or nugget of inspiration.

That's why I've written this book the way I have. It's snack-sized inspiration if you like, but there's no sell-by date. Start wherever you want to start. Read in whatever order you want to. Each chapter is self-contained, but I recognize some will have more relevance to you than others. Some may even seem to contradict others. That's intentional. I want to give you a range of insights, not some black and white, step-by-step guide to success. I deliberately want to offer contrasting perspectives, as I think it's both superficial and unhelpful to take a 'one size fits all' approach to life. So, no single chapter tells the whole story, but each will bring a perspective for you to ponder. My advice is not to race through the book. Take your time. Allow some of the ideas and insights to digest. Share what you read with others. Doing so not only helps to cement what you've read but could also stimulate further thoughts and actions.

Some of what you'll read you'll have come across before. The content will be familiar, but how I've packaged it may not be. I make no apologies for reminding you of stuff you already know. In this distraction-filled world of constant communication in all its forms, we need to be reminded of truths and insights that can easily get lost and forgotten in the constant noise of life.

There will be chapters where I explore territory which is less familiar to you. At points I'll have a perspective which perhaps seems counterintuitive or contradicts something you've come across previously. Again, I make no apologies. This book is not my attempt to simply re-hash or echo other people's ideas, but to provide some fresh food for thought, to provoke you to think more and examine familiar aspects of your life in a less familiar way. Where I can, I'll aim to inject some humour into proceedings. Life can be serious, but there's a danger we can take ourselves a little too seriously at times.

My hope is that not only will you feel better equipped to have a great life, but you'll be able to share what you've learnt to help others do the same. I think we can all play a part in helping each other live more successful, fulfilled, and happier lives.

I'd love your feedback too, so feel free to tweet @TheSumoGuy (use #greatlife) or email Paul.McGee@ theSUMOguy.com – I promise I'll reply.

Enjoy the ride.

Paul McGee

Chapter 1

DON'T TAKE MIRACLES FOR GRANTED

O K, let me start with three quick questions. When you get dressed, which shoe do you put on first, your left or your right? Secondly, when you go up a flight of stairs, which leg goes up first, your left or your right one? Finally, when you chew your food, which side of your mouth do you mostly tend to use, your left or your right?

If you're like most people you had to stop and think before giving your answer. In fact, some people are still not one hundred percent certain even when they've answered. And yet all three questions are related to things we do almost every day (except perhaps for those shoe-hating, bungalow-dwelling people on a liquid diet). In fact, we've probably done each activity thousands of times during our lives.

And that's my point.

You see, we do some things so often we don't even think about them anymore. We simply operate on autopilot.

Here's something else I'd now like you to do. Just read the following:

Richard's nickname was dig bick.

You that read wrong.

You read that wrong too.

Did it catch you out? Crazy, eh?

And the reason?

It's simply this – our brains' persistent and hardwired preoccupation for taking shortcuts. You see, our brains love to conserve energy, and as our brain cells use almost twice as much energy as any other cell in the body, the brain has developed ways to minimize effort.

One way to do so is by recognizing patterns. If everything the brain encounters is familiar – the same office, the same route to work, the same friends – or it carries out repeated routines – getting dressed, climbing stairs, or chewing food – it hums along quite happily on autopilot. The daily repetition of our lives means the brain can relax; there's no danger to be wary of, and nothing out of the ordinary going on. The brain's thinking 'Relax, I've seen this all before.' As a result, it doesn't concentrate and consciously register all the information.

Now that can be a good thing. You don't want to spend ages tiring yourself out deciding which order to get dressed in. Neither do you want to do the same when climbing stairs or chewing food. The same goes for when you're driving – you can just do it on autopilot, relax, and let your mind wander.

But that's the problem.

If we're not careful we can switch off too often. It's easy to do – to repeat over and over again regular routines, routes, and habits. But when we do, it's like living life on fast-forward.

Great Life Insight

It's easy to take for granted the richness and variety that life has to offer.

You see, to a young child everything is new, hence their sense of awe when they see animals on a farm and planes in the sky. But as these things become increasingly familiar, it's easy to take their existence for granted and to almost stop noticing them (unless, of course, you're a farmer or a plane spotter).

I'm fascinated and challenged by these words from Einstein:

> There are only two ways to live your life. One is as though nothing is a miracle. The other is as though everything is a miracle.

You know what I've realized? It's important to notice what's under your nose. To actually take time to stop, pause, and reflect. Be aware of things. Appreciate that instant running water, that hot shower, and those trees that line the street where you live.

Great Life Tip

When you're next eating, why don't you take a moment to savour the flavour?

So, rather than focusing on what you will eat next, take a moment to really enjoy what you're eating now. This is something I've started to do more. I'm taking time to appreciate the extraordinary when experiencing the ordinary. And I'm a little weird when I do so. The reason?

Well, I've started to close my eyes when I'm eating my food.

Now I don't do this throughout the whole meal obviously – that could be quite awkward, fishing around my plate with my knife and fork, searching out my next mouthful to eat. It would also be off-putting for the people I was eating with! But I do now take a couple of mouthfuls and take time to notice what I'm eating and become aware of the tastes and textures when I do so.

Now maybe we would all do that if we were in some expensive restaurant and paid a fortune for the meal. But I'm suggesting we do this on a daily basis, whatever we're eating. Trust me, cornflakes have never tasted so good.

OK, that's one example, but behind the quirky illustration there's a serious point.

Great Life Insight

It's so easy to live with the attitude 'so what's next?' rather than simply enjoying 'what's now'.

Life, even with all its challenges, is still an amazing experience. But I'm left wondering, perhaps due to over-exposure, if we've become immune to the awe-inspiring things that surround us.

Are we taking life, people, and places for granted?

The reality is, we seek out new experiences to impress us and fail to notice the miracles around us.

I love this quote from the Jewish philosopher and theologian Abraham Heschel:

> Our goal should be to live life in radical amazement … Get up in the morning and look at the world in a way that takes nothing for granted. Everything is phenomenal; everything is incredible; never treat life casually. To be spiritual is to be amazed.

You might not be aware of it, but most of us have encountered the Seven Wonders of the World. Really, we have.

Those Seven Wonders are as follows:

To see. To hear. To touch.

To taste. To feel. To laugh.

To love.

Why not take a moment to appreciate the great life you already have? We're beneficiaries of hundreds and hundreds of years of human development in relation to education, technology, health care, sanitation, entertainment, architecture, medical advancements, travel. The list is endless.

Take a moment to look around you and notice nature. Stop and stare. Get off fast-forward. We're surrounded by awe-inspiring stuff. Please don't take it all for granted.

Great Life Insight

Life is not an advert. It's the main show. Soak it in. Savour it.

And remember, if you did wake up feeling tired and miserable, you woke up. So, dust yourself down and start experiencing those Seven Wonders. And when you do so, don't take those daily miracles for granted.

Chapter 2

MAKE PEACE WITH PARADOX

Have you ever wished you were a small child again? Life was much simpler then wasn't it? I mean just think about a toddler's typical day for a moment:

Eat. Sleep. Poo. Play. Sorted.

But as we get older, life becomes increasingly complicated. Less black and white – a lot more grey. And in my own journey I've come to the conclusion that the more I know, the more I realize there's so much I don't know. As I get older I feel less confident about things I felt certain about previously.

I've struggled with that at times, as perhaps, like a lot of people, I prefer a degree of predictability over ambiguity.

When I started out as a professional speaker I was confused by the conflicting advice I received from people I respected, people who seemed to have opposite approaches to achieving their success. And my reading around human behaviour left me with a wide range of often contradictory approaches necessary to succeed in life.

Finding the 'right answer' has been a struggle, but my mate and mentor Paul once shared with me a quote from the American writer F. Scott Fitzgerald that's brought clarity to my confusion and helped me make peace with contradictions. Fitzgerald wrote:

> The test of a first-rate intelligence is the ability to hold two opposed ideas in mind at the same time and still retain the ability to function.

That's helped me a lot on my journey. It's helped me relax rather than wrestle with some issues. I've learnt to be more content with contradictions and to understand there are many different ways to achieve a great life. I now recognize that paradox pervades all aspects of life, sometimes more than we might appreciate at first. Let's take a moment to consider just how true that is.

As people, we're amazing and we can also be awful. We can be magnificent but also mediocre. We're both a masterpiece and a work in progress. We're capable of deep acts of compassion and appalling acts of cruelty. We're mature in one aspect of life and childish in another.

When we're young we like to look older, and then when we're old we want to look younger.

We're the best parents on the planet one day and the lousiest the next. As people, we can be quite simple to understand, and yet seemingly too complex to fully comprehend.

We are irrelevant, micro-sized specks of insignificance existing briefly in a vast universe. We're also people who are significant, whose lives matter. Our action or inaction makes a difference to the future of this planet, and to the people around us.

We achieve success by saying 'yes' to certain things, and yet it can also come from saying 'no' to other things. Success comes from a relentless and unwavering pursuit of your dream, and it comes from knowing when to quit and to try something else.

In life we're encouraged to develop our awareness and to notice things, and yet we're also warned against being distracted. We love the new and disregard the old. Then we pay thousands for what's old and pennies for what's new.

We develop technology to free up our time and make life easier, then become slaves to it and never switch off. We plan our holidays but not our lives. We're forever photographing or filming people, meals, and places, but not always taking time to simply appreciate the moment.

We need to be more mindful and take time out to reflect. Yet we constantly need to feel busy and be seen to be doing things. We dream of relaxing on a beach and then complain of boredom when we get there.

We say most things are common sense and yet rarely practise the sense that's so common. We complain about the long hours we work and then choose to work longer hours. We have children to be with them, then spend time away in order to support them.

You see, paradox is at the heart of who we are and what we do, and yet at times we strive to find the perfect path and discover the 'right' answer. The truth is that life is not straightforward. It's complex, messy, and not always clear cut. It's technicolour, not black and white.

Great Life Insight

Life is abundantly rich in colour, complexity, potential, and possibility.

The road to success, fulfilment, and happiness is not a straight one. It's full of twists and turns – even u-turns. Sometimes there's clarity, other times ambiguity. What makes you happy in your twenties could be different in your fifties. What works for you might not work for someone else. That's how life is. And that's OK. In fact, it's more than OK. It's liberating.

The American journalist Tony Schwartz wrote:

> Let go of certainty. Realize its opposite isn't uncertainty. It's openness, curiosity, and a willingness to embrace paradox.

I find such an outlook exciting. It frees us from a one-dimensional and one-size-fits-all approach to life.

Great Life Insight

When we embrace and make peace with paradox, it removes the straightjacket from our thinking and gives us permission to explore new horizons.

Our world pulsates with paradox, and, as a result, adds depth, richness, opportunity, and variety to our lives. In fact, life itself starts in a paradoxical way.

How? Let me explain.

I recall the birth of our son Matt. There was anxiety as we rushed to the hospital, and there was excitement at the anticipation of our first child. There was a deep sense of joy and there was physical pain, bordering on agony (my wife didn't feel too good either). There were machines and large forceps. There were doctors and nurses with reassuring smiles.

There was mess and there was magic. There was the natural consequence of the biological development of cells and chromosomes. And there was profound mystery that, somehow, my wife and I had created this new life. It was an everyday occurrence for millions of people throughout the world, but it felt special, spiritual, and unique to us.

That is the paradox of life, of our journeys. Don't fight it. Make peace with it.

Chapter 3

REMEMBER YOU'RE OK

I remember as a small child falling in the school playground. I was around seven years old. I can still recall it vividly and was convinced there was masses of blood pouring from my mouth (although it was probably just saliva).

My mates gathered round to check if I was OK. They also came to congratulate me. I'd fallen whilst scoring a goal for my team – a rare feat on my part. Then one of the lunch time supervisors (although this was the early 1970s, so we called them dinner ladies) came over to see what the commotion was about.

She assessed the damage and reassuringly and confidently declared 'You're OK.'

My crying, which was so intense it even made my shoulders shake, became more subdued.

'I hear you scored for your team. Well done' she said. 'Now let's just give that mouth and those knees a little wash and then you can go and score some more.'

My sobbing came to a standstill, and after a brief wash in the toilets I was back in the game.

So, what's this memory from a lifetime ago got to do with you?

Well, I think we all need to be reminded at times that we're OK.

That, despite our struggles, our falls, and our pain, fundamentally, at our very core as human beings, we need to recognize and accept we're OK.

However, the reality is we often struggle through life desperately trying to prove our worth and gain acceptance.

Why?

Because we actually live in a world that plays on us not feeling OK. A world that magnifies our insecurities and can make us feel unhappy about who we are, what we do, and what we look like. But relax, because there's some good news. There's a product or experience that can remedy and fix all that.

At a price of course.

Some parts of the media can send us mixed messages. On one hand, we're being told how amazing and wonderful we are, and to purchase an expensive product 'because we're worth it'. But equally, we're being bombarded with messages that we need fixing, that we're falling short, not looking good enough, and need to keep in touch with the in-crowd.

You see, from a marketing perspective it's crucial to create in each of us a sense of dissatisfaction or desire that can only be satisfied by a particular product.

The underlying message being 'You're OK if ...'

So, rather than feeling good about who we are and the amazing potential we all possess, we can be made to feel inadequate and encouraged to believe that our main aim in life should be to eradicate our imperfections and refuse to accept our flaws.

Because unless you do, you're not OK.

And this can slowly entice us into the *'lure for more'* trap, where we think having more, doing more, being more is the only way to feel good about ourselves.

But it can become a never-ending cycle, and our desire for approval and acceptance can lead us on an endless quest to prove our worth both to ourselves and others.

Great Life Insight

There's a big difference between wanting to learn, grow, and improve, compared with feeling continually inadequate for not being perfect.

Now please don't get me wrong, I completely understand that dissatisfaction drives us and humanity as a whole to want to improve our lives. Hey, the very reason you're reading this book could be driven by a desire to improve and develop yourself. I get that. But . . .

Great Life Insight

When it comes to improving ourselves, let's start from a position of self-acceptance rather than self-loathing.

Trust me, I've entertained self-loathing for a long time. For years it was my constant companion, particularly in relation to my appearance. I focused on my flaws incessantly and lived with an enduring belief that I wasn't OK.

But here's the thing:

No matter how hard I tried to improve myself, I never seemed to arrive at a place of feeling whole and OK. So, I know from my own painful experience that this is not the path to travel in order to increase our sense of success, fulfilment, and happiness. In fact, such a journey weakens our wellbeing and can sow the seeds of poor mental health.

So instead, let's start with the attitude 'I'm OK and ...'

Recognize that we all have some flaws and failings we might want to work on, but let's also accept they're part of our humanity. It's what makes us who we are and what makes us unique. In fact, in some cases our flaws are part of our appeal. Think about it for a moment – how appealing would the Tower of Pisa be if it wasn't leaning?

Now I'm not here to make excuses for inappropriate behaviour. Neither am I saying let's put aside our desire to grow and develop. Far from it.

But I am saying . . .

Great Life Insight

Let's begin with the truth that there's already something amazing about being human, and therefore something amazing about being you.

I think we're best served by identifying what's going well, what's good about who we are, and building upon it, rather than focusing all our attention on what's wrong and how to fix it.

Just think about this for a moment:

Of all the millions of sperm released, only one got to fertilize the egg.

That's why you're you. You won the race.

And you did a pretty good job being born too – you even got a certificate to prove it.

When you realize you're OK, you're less likely to quit when you fall. You're less likely to want a pity party and some sympathy, and more likely to want to dust yourself down, clean yourself up, and get on with the game.

So please don't waste your time and energy trying to be perfect. Yes, pursue your desires for improvement. Strive for excellence. Develop your abilities. Grow in your understanding. But do so from a place of self-acceptance and acknowledgement that, however flawed and fragile you may feel at times, you really are OK.

Chapter 4

FOLLOW THE SAFETY ANNOUNCEMENTS

I get to travel on planes a lot. I'm always fascinated how often I'm called over for a random spot check when going through security. Maybe there's just something about me that looks random, or perhaps I have one of those faces that says 'Pick me!' Whatever the reason, it's nice to be noticed.

A security scanner in Colorado once revealed there was some anomaly that they'd discovered in my groin area. I felt rather concerned until they revealed I'd left a small piece of tissue in my trouser pocket.

That's my story anyway.

Having safely navigated my way through security and duty free, my next big task is boarding the plane. I do so in the vain hope that the overhead lockers won't be full, and I'll be sat next to a petite person who has no desire to do anything with their elbows except keep them out of my personal space and who remembered to put on deodorant.

Then comes that awkward moment.

The safety announcements.

It's no exaggeration to say I've heard them hundreds of times. When they're shown on a video screen I feel less guilty about reading my paper and not paying full attention, but when the safety announcements are being delivered by a member of the cabin crew and they're stood in the aisle close to me, I'm overcome with a sense of schoolboy guilt and find myself hanging on every word. (And I'm always left wondering how many passing fishermen I'd be able to attract the attention of with my whistle were the plane to crash.)

But there's an interesting part of the safety announcements that always gets me thinking.

'If there is a drop in cabin pressure, the oxygen masks will come down. Please secure your own mask first, before helping others.'

Wise advice, hey?

Put your own oxygen mask on first before helping others.

Actually, I think that's a great metaphor for life.

You see, the word 'inspire' means 'to breathe life into'. The problem is that things such as people, bureaucracy, change, finances, uncertainty, and politics, to name just a few, can all suck the life out of you at times. Agree?

Great Life Insight

The challenge is so many of us are trying to be a hero to others that we often fail to be a hero to ourselves.

We can spend our time putting on other people's oxygen masks but neglect to put on our own.

Now I'm not suggesting you stop helping others. For instance, if you've got young children I'm not advising you start survival training when they're toddlers and get them to cook their own meals and change their own nappies (although the thought is quite appealing).

But I am saying make yourself and your own needs a priority rather than an afterthought.

By doing so, not only will you benefit, but ultimately so will others.

> ## Great Life Insight
>
> Self-care isn't selfish – it's the key to our success and sanity.

But I wonder how tired and worn out we make ourselves in our desire to meet other people's needs to the exclusion of our own?

The reality is, you can't pour from an empty cup. You can't give what you haven't got.

Try to do so and, rather than feeling a sense of reward from helping others, you'll begin to feel a sense of resentment. If you do feel you've got to that point, trust me, it's time to put your own oxygen mask on first.

So, is self-care simple and easy to do? Possibly not. Which means you have to plan and prioritize it. What that looks like in reality will be different for each of us.

In my world, putting on my own oxygen mask means taking time out to read. It means scheduling in some form of exercise four or five times a week. It means not dealing with work emails after 7 p.m. It means going for some fresh air for a few minutes during the day just by myself. It means rarely driving for more than two hours without a 15-minute break. It also means resting well and realizing surviving regularly on less than six hours of sleep a night doesn't make me Superman – it makes me stupid. Crucially, it means prioritizing some fun time with family and friends.

Great Life Insight

Don't hope for happy times. Plan them.

So, what does putting your own oxygen mask on first look like for you? What breathes life into you? Pause for a moment and think of your top three things.

When did you last do them?

Whatever they are, remember to make them a priority. In a nutshell, *'Plan Happy.'*

Don't leave it to chance – make it a conscious choice.

And make sure you follow those safety announcements – not just for a safe flight, but also for a great life.

Chapter 5

QUIT PLAYING THE GAME YOU'LL NEVER WIN

I enjoy time on my own. As I work away from home a great deal, a lot of it can be spent in hotels, and at least one night a week is inevitably spent in the room of a well-known hotel chain, where I often ponder whether their 'Good night guarantee' will include a glass of milk and a bedtime story.

But I can only cope with so much 'alone time'. There are limits to how much of my own company I enjoy before I need to reach out and engage with others. The degree of that need to be with others can depend on our personality, but whether you're an extrovert or an introvert, people are relational by nature. We need each other. In fact, we were born to bond.

As we grow up we find our identity within the context of our relationships with others. We develop our behaviour by observing what other people do and we learn what is and isn't socially acceptable by picking up social cues from those around us. In other words, we spend our lives comparing ourselves to others.

So, travelling naked is usually off the agenda (although it would make going through airport security so much quicker and easier) and although as a toddler you could get away with throwing your food everywhere and rubbing it in your hair, people are perhaps less understanding of you carrying on that tradition into adulthood.

So, in a sense we have to compare ourselves with others. We simply cannot exist in isolation. To do so would be devastating for our development both socially and emotionally.

However . . .

Great Life Insight

Our problems occur when we place too much importance on constantly comparing ourselves with others and allow it to dominate our lives.

And living today, it's never been so easy and so tempting to do. You see, go back 200,000 years and our ancestors were usually part of a group that numbered no more than 150.

Now, with the rise of social media and the internet, our tribe is over 7 billion.

In fact, it's argued that our exposure to social media has heightened the potential for us to feel inadequate and insecure. And it's so easy for that to happen isn't it?

I'm sure, like most people, when I post a picture of myself on social media I'm not trawling through my photos hunting for the one where I look especially awful (trust me, there are countless ones to choose from).

'Oh yes, that angle really highlights all three of my chins and my sagging stomach; I'll use that as my profile pic.'

I guess, like most people, I'm wanting to post a picture that presents me in a positive light. Who doesn't? (However, I don't go as far as Kim Kardashian, whose tip for taking a selfie is to take around 300 pictures and then choose the best one.)

But some people take that further don't they? Their aim is to present a photoshopped version of their lives that portrays nothing but positivity. Hey, that's their choice, and in a world where negative news dominates it can be quite uplifting to read about the good things happening in people's lives.

But here's the problem:

Great Life Insight

The danger is we compare our unedited lives with the edited version of someone else's.

The trouble is, we don't get to see their whole album, just the images they want us to see.

The ones enhanced with filters. The ones that paint a heavily distorted picture of people's lives.

The challenge is, when we constantly compare our lives to those of others, it's not a recipe for feeling fulfilled and happy.

You see, with 7 billion people on the planet, I don't care how good you are at something, there's bound to be someone who can do it better. Maybe you do have an amazing body, but there'll always be someone with better-defined abs and bigger biceps. There'll always be someone richer than you, fitter than you, faster than you. There'll always be someone who's luckier than you, or more talented than you.

So please stop and get off the comparison conveyor belt, because it could be damaging your mental health.

And if you haven't done so already, check out the chapter 'Remember You're OK'. If you've already read it, read it again.

Here's the deal:

Great Life Insight

We need to recognize our intrinsic worth as people is not based on how we measure up to others.

Remember, we're all running our own unique race, within the context of our own set of circumstances and personal history. And we'll enjoy the journey a whole lot more when we focus our energies on creating a better life and adding value to others rather than constantly comparing our lives to other people's.

Great Life Tip

Start by appreciating who you are, rather than regretting who you aren't.

The bottom line is this: every minute you spend wishing you had someone else's life is a minute spent wasting yours.

And please do yourself a favour: don't compare your Chapter 3 with someone else's Chapter 28. We all start in different places and we're all at different stages, so get on with living your life and leave others to lead theirs.

Now by all means be inspired by other people. Be challenged by what they've achieved, but just remember other people's success doesn't make you a failure. So, strive to be *your* best, rather than only being satisfied when you're *the* best.

Finally, here are two things in relation to the comparison game I've learnt from my time on this planet.

Firstly:

Great Life Insight

We tend to overglamorize what we don't have and undervalue what we do have.

I would read that again if I were you, because I think it's so important we grasp this fact.

Secondly, other people's grass may appear greener, but quite often it's been fertilized with bullshit. And even if it hasn't, get watering your own garden rather than envying someone else's.

So here's my good night guarantee.

Want to enjoy a great life? Then get on with creating one and quit constantly comparing yourself to others. Because that's a game you'll never win.

Chapter 6

LIVE
LIFE ON
PURPOSE

Alfred Nobel was a man of many talents: a chemist, an engineer, an inventor, and a businessman.

Busy bloke, eh?

However, of all the roles he played in life, he was probably best known for inventing dynamite. And I guess that's what he would have always been remembered for – until something rather strange happened.

In 1888, Alfred's brother Ludvig died. Now what's strange about that you ask? Nothing.

But here's the interesting bit:

The next day, several newspapers published obituaries not of Ludvig but of Alfred instead.

Think about that for a moment. That must have been a pretty weird experience: to open the newspapers and not only read of your own death, but also other people's memories of your life. And despite Alfred's many achievements, guess what? It was his invention of dynamite that stole the headlines.

One headline summed up his life in six words: '*The merchant of death is dead.*'

The obituary went on to say, 'Dr. Alfred Nobel, who became rich by finding ways to kill more people faster than ever before, died yesterday.'

Some legacy to leave, hey? Alfred Nobel, a man who never married or had any children, would always be remembered as 'the merchant of death'.

Except, of course, Alfred was still very much alive, and a bit like Ebenezer Scrooge in *A Christmas Carol* he'd been given an insight most of us will never have – what people really think of you once you're dead.

Having read the obituary, Alfred wanted to leave a better legacy. He wanted to be remembered for something positive, and that's what inspired him to bequeath most of his rather large estate when he died eight years later to establishing the Nobel prizes. Yes, he was still the inventor of dynamite, but now he was leaving a different legacy.

So, what's all this got to do with you and me? Quite a lot, actually.

I'm pretty sure as most of us plough on in our day-to-day lives we rarely, if ever, give thought to the legacy we're creating, or the memories people will have of us once we're gone. I guess that's fairly understandable – but doing so could actually prove invaluable.

You see, as I move into my mid-fifties I do think about my legacy more – my wife and I even talk about our funerals. Now you might accuse us of being morbid, but I like to think it's a gentle reminder that, however long we have on this planet, we're not invincible, and each of us does have a sell-by date. And, sadly, for some that sell-by date arrives sooner than planned.

So how does that relate to success, fulfilment, and happiness? Why should thinking about your death help you lead a great life? Good question.

Here's my answer:

Great Life Insight

People who have a strong sense of purpose and have found meaning to their lives are usually the most fulfilled.

Interestingly, that's not dependent on people's life circumstances. I've known charity workers give up all the trappings of a comfortable Western lifestyle to work with some of the poorest, most deprived people on the planet, and who are incredibly happy.

The reason?

They have a strong sense of purpose – they believe they're making a difference and that what they're doing matters.

And you don't have to do anything extreme to find such fulfilment. I also know elderly people who now have grandchildren and have discovered a fresh meaning and purpose to their lives. My friend Matt bought a dog recently – and although he never lost his mojo, it's fair to say he's got a new spring in his step since becoming a dog owner.

Equally, I've met some incredibly wealthy people who have no sense of meaning and purpose. They pursue pleasure but ultimately still feel empty inside. What I've come to realize is:

Great Life Insight

It's purpose, more than pounds in your pocket, that brings the greatest life satisfaction.

Here's our challenge though: we can quickly (and perhaps unquestioningly) step onto the treadmill of life and end up living it on autopilot.

Great Life Insight

We can become a consumer of things and a collector of experiences but never give much thought to what our lives are about.

Perhaps it's time to get off that treadmill for a moment and ask ourselves some important questions. It might be worthwhile jotting down your answers to the following:

- What kind of person do I want to become? (To answer this, think about three things you would want people to say about you at your funeral.)

- Who truly matters to me? (Remember, purpose can come from the role you play in the lives of others.)

- What do I care about?

- What energizes me?

- What makes me angry?

- What am I doing when I feel happiest?

- How do I want to behave towards myself, others, and the world around me?

You see, it's so easy to be caught up in the minutiae of life and lose sight of the bigger picture. In doing so we can confuse our priorities and overlook what really matters.

Maybe it's just me, but I've got a funny feeling you won't be hearing the following at anyone's funeral:

- They had great abs.

- Their biceps were amazing.

- They didn't have an ounce of cellulite on them.

- They had an incredible kitchen.

- They had amazing teeth.

- Their car could do 0–60 in less than three seconds.

I'm not suggesting that all the above are unimportant. Taking pride in your appearance and enjoying some of life's pleasures is great. But I don't believe that's the whole story. If it is for you, fine. But for many it's not. Certainly not when they actually stop and think about their life and what truly matters.

From my conversations with people who have lived a long and full life I've discovered the following:

Great Life Insight

It's not about who has the most toys, it's who has the most joys that really makes a great life.

And what seems to be the key to most people's fulfilment is not the possessions they acquired (nice though they might be) but the relationships they developed and the sense of purpose they had from what they did in life, no matter how small or insignificant that might have looked to others. (Hey, if you live on your own caring for your cat, that still gives you a purpose for getting out of bed.)

Of course, we're all different. We're not all on the same journey. Your purpose will be different to mine. What brings each of us pleasure will vary, but eventually we will all take our leave of this planet.

Now for some that's the end of the story. Others believe there's something even better to follow. But whatever your beliefs, let's just make sure we experience life before death.

Let's find a sense of meaning and purpose in who we are and in what we do. In the words of Pericles, the Greek statesman and orator, let's remember this:

> What you leave behind is not what is engraved in stone monuments, but what is woven into the lives of others.

Alfred Nobel changed his legacy by finding a new purpose in life. And your great life comes from living out your purpose or making sure you find one.

I wonder, if there was a headline that summarized your life in six words, what would it say?

Chapter 7

ARE YOU FAILING ANY OF THE 7 CS?

There are several signs that indicate you've reached middle age. One day you'll thank me for alerting you to them. In my case, my ear lobes started to get hairier, my eyebrows became wilder, and my nasal hair had a growth spurt. Bizarre really.

Oh, and there's something else too. I started visiting garden centres on a regular basis. Now I know that garden centres are not the exclusive domain of the middle-aged and elderly, but in my experience, we do tend to form the majority of the visitors.

One thing I've noticed when I buy a new plant is that it invariably comes with a small card. Basically, it's an idiot's guide on how to care for the plant in order for it to thrive and flourish. Each card is different depending on the plant – a 'one size fits all' approach to plant care is a definite no-no.

Now this got me thinking – wouldn't it be wonderful if, when you met someone, they presented you with a card which highlighted how best to treat them. Or when a child was born you were magically presented with an instruction manual on how best to bring them up – and each instruction manual was tailored specifically to that child. Life would be so much easier wouldn't it?

Of course, the reality is when it comes to dealing with people we often muddle through, make it up as we go along, get advice from friends, and simply hope for the best.

Which is why I developed my '7 Cs to Thrive' model.

So, whether you're raising children, managing people, or simply want a steer in how to help yourself and others thrive and flourish in life, you will find focusing on the 7 Cs hugely beneficial.

It's born out of my background in psychology, human resources, and working with over one thousand organizations, and is a simple tool to help assess seven factors that contribute to thriving in life. Now although all seven factors can relate to any area of your life, it's perhaps easier to explore them within a work context (be that paid or unpaid). If you're not in work, then still go through the exercise and see how these factors relate to your own particular situation. As you do, make a mental note of the ones you feel generally happy about, as well as those that cause you some concern.

The 7 Cs are as follows:

1. **Clarity**. You are clear on what is expected of you in your role and why what you do is important. You're clear on how your role helps contribute towards the bigger picture and you don't need to guess about what's expected of you in terms of behaviour or performance. You're clear on what success looks like and clear on your purpose.

2. **Competent**. You have the skills, knowledge, and training to do your job well. You know how to access support if and when your skills need developing. In a nutshell, you're good at what you do.

3. **Confident**. You have self-belief in who you are and what you are able to do. This is based not solely on how you feel, but also on feedback from others, particularly your manager (if you have one).

4. **Comfortable**. You feel at home and at ease with those you work with. You feel part of the team and are comfortable sharing your ideas and, when necessary, expressing your concerns.

5. **Challenge**. You feel an appropriate amount of challenge in what you do. You recognize there may be busier or quieter periods of work, but generally speaking you feel neither overwhelmed nor underwhelmed with work.

6. **Cared for**. You feel others around you care for you and your wellbeing. You don't feel taken for granted but appreciated. You know when you need emotional support you have people you can turn to.

7. **Control**. You have a degree of control in what you do, or in how you do it. You are still able to think for yourself and able to use your own initiative and judgement. You may have processes to follow, but you can still put your mark on certain aspects of the job. You are not micromanaged.

Take some time to reflect on each of these seven areas. Which, if any, need particular attention from you? If you had to score each factor on a scale from 1–10 (1 = low, 10 = high) in terms of satisfaction, would there be any you would score below 6? If so, is there anything you can do to address the issue, or perhaps someone you can talk to?

Having used this tool with organizations over the last couple of years, it's proved invaluable in helping people to pinpoint areas they have needed to address in order to increase their job satisfaction and improve their job performance. It's a great tool to help facilitate conversations between managers and their team. It has also crucially highlighted why some people are not fully satisfied in their current role and given them the opportunity to address the issue and work out the best way forward.

Great Life Insight

People are like plants. They only thrive in certain environments.

The 7 Cs to Thrive model is a tool both for conversation and reflection. If you would like to explore it further, specifically in relation to work, please visit www.thrivethe system.co.uk.

I believe the tool also has a wider application to life, and by addressing the 7 Cs you can help increase your own life satisfaction. A low score in any of those areas could explain why you're not feeling fulfilled or happy in life. For example, a low score in 'Clarity' could indicate you feel a lack of direction or sense of purpose in your life at present. A low score in 'Cared for' could indicate you feel taken for granted by others or perhaps don't feel you have anyone to turn to for support.

I believe it could also be a tool that, when adapted, could be used with children to help create an environment and set of relationships where they are able to thrive and flourish. And perhaps parents could also use it to help themselves identify where they need support. For instance, none of us are born competent parents. So that could be an area where we need some help and advice, which, in turn, could lead to us feeling more confident.

If your scores are high in all seven areas, then that's great news. Your goal is to see how you can continue to maintain those high scores. If some of your scores are low, you now have the opportunity to do something about it. If you choose not to, you'll be like that plant that is perhaps doing OK but would thrive so much more if given the appropriate care and the right environment. Ultimately, it's your life and your call but I genuinely hope you find the 7 Cs will help you and others to thrive in life.

Right, I'm off to groom my eyebrows.

Chapter 8

TATTOO THIS ON YOUR TORSO

My daughter Ruth and I have similar personalities. We both enjoy being the centre of attention, we can be loud, and we love meeting new people and travelling . . . preferably to somewhere sunny.

There are differences, however.

High heels, make up, and handbags are not high on my agenda, and my tolerance for alcohol is much lower than hers. I also have far fewer followers on Instagram.

There's something else we have in common though. We like quotes – particularly ones that inspire and make us think. One that I especially like is by the late French novelist Anaïs Nin:

> We do not see things as they are, we see things
> as we are.

However, I misquoted this to Ruth, my version being 'We see the world not as it is, but as we are.'

Ruth loved it. So much so she had it tattooed on her torso.

My version that is, not Anaïs Nin's.

Sorry Anaïs.

Great Life Insight

It's our outlook on life that determines what we see.

Or, to put it another way, you don't believe what you see, you see what you believe.

Let me explain.

An elderly relative of mine now lives on his own, having lost his partner of 25 years. We were chatting recently, and he said: 'It's a sad, sad world out there Paul.' And unfortunately, through his eyes, because of his loss, it is.

But that same world he views as sad is seen by someone else as a place of joy and opportunity.

The reality, of course, is that neither view is right or wrong. It's simply a view.

Now here's the intriguing bit: strange as it may seem, our brains have the ability to find what we're looking for. Really, they do.

For instance, if you're changing your car, have you noticed that suddenly you start spotting the make and model you're thinking of buying everywhere? Or have you ever put your home up for sale and then started noticing 'For sale' signs everywhere? The same goes if you or your partner are pregnant. You start noticing other people who are pregnant, and your awareness of the world of babies is suddenly awakened. True?

In a nutshell, what's important to you, you start to notice. And what you believe about the world, you start to notice too.

The same is true in terms of how you see yourself. For example, some people, for a whole variety of reasons, see themselves as victims of fate and circumstances, and see the world as an unfair place. And because they see themselves this way, they believe they're powerless to do anything to improve their situation.

The result?

Life becomes a self-fulfilling prophecy.

Great Life Insight

If I choose to focus on what I'm unhappy or dissatisfied about, my brain will dutifully oblige and seek out evidence to support this view.

But now for the good news – my brain will also help me notice the positive and good things in my life – if that's what I'm looking for.

So why don't our brains notice the whole picture and give us a balanced perspective on life?

Good question.

The fact is, our brain can only consciously notice and retain a small amount of information, so in order to avoid cognitive overload it filters out information it considers irrelevant or unimportant. So, if you believe the world is a sad place, your brain isn't going to start arguing with you and say 'Hey, just hang on a minute, there's actually loads to feel thankful and grateful for, just let me show you.'

That's not its place.

Great Life Insight

From a survival perspective, your brain has a built-in bias to notice negatives and spot any potential threats. Its primary purpose is to keep you alive, not make you happy.

So how do you counter this bias? Quite simply, we need to consciously and deliberately notice the positives, otherwise we end up being blind to them, or simply taking them for granted. Some people do seem quite well predisposed to do this naturally, but if you're like me then that's not always the case.

You see, for someone known as a motivational or inspirational speaker I have to confess I am, by nature and disposition, a little negative and prone to anxiety.

I was once described by a comedian as Mr Dour Face (although to be fair I had heard earlier that Bradford had lost at Wembley to Millwall). I'm just not like my wife, who, from the moment she wakes, seems to have an air of cheerfulness and joy about her (and that's despite being married to me for over 30 years).

I actually have to make a conscious decision to notice the positives and remind myself of all I have to be grateful for. This is why I'm now so passionate about what I speak and write about. I know this stuff works. I've experienced the benefits. Without it I would just be a miserable bloke from Manchester.

So, here's the deal: it's not your life that makes you happy – it's what you think about your life.

See the world as a sad, dark, and miserable place and it will be.

See it as a challenging place that still pulsates with opportunity and beauty and that is what you will find.

Great Life Insight

'When you change the way you look at things, the things you look at change.' – Wayne Dyer

You might not want to tattoo the phrase 'We see the world not as it is, but as we are' on your torso, but do imprint it on your mind.

Because maybe your life is already great – it's just that you've not been looking for what's actually great about it.

Chapter 9

MOLEHILLS MATTER . . . MASSIVELY

My friend and colleague Ed is a generally laid-back kind of guy. Few things seem to stress him, but there is one thing that gets him agitated and angry. And that's when you mention moles. (Of the animal variety.)

To me, moles, with their velvety fur and small eyes and feet, seem rather cute. Not to Ed they're not. You see, Ed is a keen gardener and was extremely proud of his immaculate lawn when he moved to his new house.

That's until Mickey the Mole and his mates arrived on the scene.

They just started doing what moles do: eating worms, building tunnels, and, of course, creating molehills. For Ed, though, this meant all-out war. You see, for small creatures they don't half make a difference to Ed's lawn, even if the molehills they create are only small.

Ed's experience got me thinking. Small things can make a big impact.

However, we're often encouraged to believe that if we want to see real change in our lives we must make massive changes. In fact, in some circles incremental change is even mocked. To an extent, I do understand where people are coming from.

My mate John certainly does.

He wanted to lose weight and decided a gradual, slow approach to weight loss was not motivating enough. So, he decided on impulse to stop eating meat and chocolate ever again. And he kept to his word.

For four days.

Before you knew it, he was once again tucking into juicy steaks and devouring chocolate like it was about to be made illegal.

You see, I think that's the dilemma many of us face. We want big goals to motivate and excite us and to reach for the stars, but then become quickly demoralized by our lack of progress and end up quitting.

On the other hand, slow and steady progress doesn't really excite us. Yet, perhaps surprisingly, it could still make us happy.

Don't believe me? Well check this out.

Research from Harvard Professor Teresa Amabile indicates that life satisfaction is 22% more likely for those with a steady stream of minor accomplishments compared to those who express interest in only major achievements. But we often convince ourselves achieving only big goals makes us happy when that's not always the case.

In fact, there's plenty of evidence to support the idea that molehills matter.

In their best-selling book *Switch: How to Change Things when Change is Hard* (a superb book, by the way), Dan and Chip Heath talk about the importance of 'shrinking the change' so it's seen as doable, and also highlight the need to go for quick wins no matter how small.

The reality is, nothing motivates like success.

Great Life Insight

There is magic in thinking big, but there's also motivation in starting small.

In my experience it's those small wins that not only give us momentum but can also give us the motivation to maintain our progress.

Here's how it's worked with me.

Since being a child I have dreamt of writing a book. I must have been around six years old when I told my classmates I was going to write one. I even had a title for it – 'Death Won't Die'. Clearly, I was a confident, if rather morbid, child.

So where did I begin in my quest to fulfil my big dream and become a published author? I started with the molehills. I wrote letters to newspapers and went on to write articles for my student magazine. I designed and wrote marketing material for events at university. People liked what I wrote. Newspapers published my letters.

However, my first book wasn't published until I was 31 – 25 years after I initially said I would write one.

Now I'm not saying that you'll have to persevere for 25 years to achieve your goal, but you do have to start somewhere and remind yourself that molehills matter.

In the world of sport, coaches like David Brailsford and Sir Clive Woodward talk about 'marginal gains' – small changes that, when added together, can make a big difference. Many businesses have adopted the Kaizen method, which is an approach of continuous improvement often brought about by small, incremental changes. It was first practised in Japanese businesses after the Second World War and it's a philosophy that's now spread throughout the world and achieved great success.

Great Life Insight

Small but repeated actions add up over time.

Here's another example from my own life of the power of small actions.

I believe I have two superpowers. Firstly, I can appear invisible – particularly when in a bar trying to get served. No matter how long I wait to order, I seem to disappear from the sight of bar staff.

My second superpower is that I'm very skilled at putting on weight quickly (although with the right clothing I disguise it quite well). My metabolism isn't slow – it actually seems to be on strike most of the time. I have been dieting on and off since I was eleven and seen rapid weight loss before piling it all back on again.

Five years ago, I realized not only did I talk about SUMO, but if my large consumption of carbs continued, I was in danger of beginning to look like one (and seriously, I do not look good in a thong of any size).

But here was my problem: I had become disillusioned with diets.

So, I decided to change my strategy and take the molehill approach. I went for small wins.

My Achilles heel is that I absolutely adore bread. I eat loads of it, particularly if we have a few slices left that are reaching their sell-by date.

Why?

Because I also hate waste.

So here was my small action to reduce my bread intake. Buy sliced bread and put it in the freezer, which was no big deal, as I'm mainly toasting it anyway. And if I'm wanting a sandwich I'll defrost a couple of slices. It takes 30 seconds.

I also make a rule when I'm travelling and staying at a hotel – never eat two slices of toast at breakfast. One and a half is fine, but not two.

Other small changes to my diet included reducing slightly the portion size of the cereal I eat and enjoying fat chips as a treat rather than as a birthright.

Here's how the molehill approach has helped me with my fitness.

As I stay in many hotels without gyms, I started doing press-ups. I began with 30. I now do three lots of 30 on most days. That's 90 in total. Which is no big deal. But that's 630 press-ups in a week, and 2520 a month.

Small actions repeated over time add up, in whatever area of life you apply them.

So, I wonder where in your life you could take this approach?

You see, here's the score my friend. How do you move forward? One step at a time. How do you lose weight? One kilo at a time. How do you write a book? One page at a time. How do you build a relationship? One day at a time.

Great Life Insight

In a world obsessed with speed, never forget things of real worth and value take time.

Now am I saying this is the only approach to achieving success? Of course not. But perhaps our unhappiness and lack of fulfilment have been due to setting big goals and then not knowing how to achieve them. If that's you, start small.

Great Life Tip

Focus on progress, not perfection.

Want to have a great life?

Then start by doing the small but critical things you need to do every single day. Most of the time, life changes with small, consistent steps that gradually take us where we want to go.

And those small actions add up.

Molehills matter. Massively.

Just don't mention that to Ed.

Chapter 10

WHY FEAR ISN'T ALWAYS YOUR ENEMY

I recently came across some research that I found both sad and surprising. According to a Gallup poll, only 13% of people are actively engaged at work. So, I feel incredibly fortunate, as I'm definitely part of that 13%. You see, my work is also my hobby. I'm passionate about it. I've been consuming personal development books for over 30 years now – not out of duty, but out of desire. I've also heard some of the top speakers in the world on the subject of motivation and success. Some have lived up to their hype, others less so.

However, whatever the quality of the speaker, when it comes to the subject of success they all seem to have one thing in common – they give the subject of 'fear' a hard time. The typical message seems to be if you can conquer your fears then you'll be able to achieve anything in life.

It's inspiring stuff and I genuinely believe that many people have been helped by hearing such speakers, at least in the short term. I'm never going to knock the opportunity to receive a large dose of positivity. But here's my issue:

I'm just not sure if fear is always the bad guy.

What holds us back from fulfilling our potential and living a great life is a whole host of factors. I don't believe that you're some sad loser because, in certain situations, you've felt scared and uncomfortable. In fact, I'm going to suggest the complete opposite.

Rather than seeing fear as your enemy, you'd actually be justified in seeing fear as your friend. But with one strong caveat:

Like all friendships, you need to work out the intricacies of your relationship.

So, fear can be your friend? Really?

Yes. Let me explain.

To do so, let's meet a couple of characters from one of my previous books, Bob and Frank.

Here's a bit about Bob and Frank. They actually lived over 100,000 years ago. They're part of a tribe called *Homo sapiens*. Bob is a laid-back optimist. He fears very little. He hardly ever worries about anything, except if he's not eaten for several days. Even then he's convinced his luck will soon change, and if it doesn't he's pretty sure his wife Brenda will rustle up one of her famous berry and dried grass stews, cooked in the bone juices of that woolly mammoth they killed a few weeks ago.

Frank, on the other hand, is nothing like Bob. In fact, he's the complete opposite.

He's always tense when they go out on a hunting expedition. He's hyper cautious. Some would say he sees the glass half empty, whilst others aren't even sure if he's got a glass.

Vigilant is his middle name. (His parents argued for ages over that one.)

When Bob and Frank are out hunting together, Bob remains confident that if a predator does attack them they'll go for Frank because they can see fear in his eyes.

Now let's fast forward a few weeks.

You're at a funeral.

It's Bob's.

His wife Brenda wipes away a tear as Frank says a few words about his recently deceased friend.

'Anyone want Bob's "No Fear" T-shirt?' he asks the rest of the tribe.

Here's the deal: Bob had something wrong with his wiring. His constant laid-back, optimistic attitude to life was actually a recipe for his death. It made him a sitting duck for sabre-toothed tigers, or a tasty meal for woolly mammoths.

Frank, on the other hand, was more fortunate. His ancestors passed down to him the life-saving emotion called fear.

Frank never wore Bob's 'No Fear' T-shirt. He preferred the one that said:

> I'd rather be fearful and alive than complacent and dead.

(Admittedly it's not as short and snappy as Bob's.)

Now let's be clear. Our relationship with fear has gone a little haywire in recent years, but its initial purpose was to alert us to danger and prepare the body to deal with a potential attack or threat. The bottom line is this:

Great Life Insight

As a species, we owe our very existence to fear.

Fear is, in fact, a normal emotion but unfortunately there are times when it becomes a well-meaning but rather dominating friend. It can be oversensitive, and if you feed it too much negative news that will only increase its strength and hold over you.

However, living life with absolutely no fear is pretty dumb – if you want to live a long life, that is.

So maybe it's time to be a little less harsh on ourselves and recognize that feeling some degree of fear is not a sign of weakness. It's a sign of being alive. It's an emotion that can stop you doing stupid things and putting your life at risk.

That's the good news, but the problem is some fears are completely irrational and have the potential to prevent you from making the most of your life.

So how can you tell whether fear is helpful or unhelpful? Well, to answer that let's use the FEAR approach.

As you go through this process, think about an issue in your life that might be causing you to feel fearful or anxious and then go through each step.

Face it. Clarify what the issue is, don't hide from it. Get whatever your issue is out into the open. You might even find it helpful to write it down.

Examine. What are the reasons for the feelings you're experiencing? Are you concerned about other people's opinions? Being rejected? Take time to explore the reasons for your feelings. Are they justified, or have you blown things out of proportion?

Accept. Anxiety and adrenaline are perfectly normal in certain situations, so don't fight them, accept them.

Reframe it. Ask yourself, 'What's another way of looking at this issue?' or 'How important will this be in six months' time?' Perhaps chatting to other people and getting their perspective would be useful to help you do this.

Now fear is a big topic, and this is a short chapter. So, if it has really become a debilitating issue for you then you may want to seek professional help.

Just remember this:

Great Life Insight

Fear's main aim is to protect you – just be careful it doesn't always direct you.

As the adventurer Bear Grylls says,

> Being brave isn't the absence of fear. Being brave is having that fear but finding a way through it.

So, see it as a well-meaning friend – and not your enemy. And make sure it's the backseat passenger in your life – it's not meant to be the driver. Not if you want to live a great life, that is.

Chapter 11

DON'T LEAVE YOUR DREAMS IN THE BIN

It was a momentous day for me when I signed off invalidity benefit and became self-employed. Three years of illness had taken its toll not only on my finances but also my self-esteem. It felt good to no longer feel awkward when I met people and they asked, 'So what do you do?' Having an illness with no visible outward symptoms and being only in my early twenties had often been met with a surprised response when I replied 'Actually I don't work. I'm ill and on invalidity benefit.'

But that was about to change. It felt good to say I was self-employed, and it felt even better when I bigged myself up and said, 'I run my own business.'

However, the reality was I had no clients, no money, and no equipment. My international headquarters doubled as a bedroom. I had an old desk, a telephone, and a double bed. It was a bit of a challenge. Particularly for Bob and Linda in the double bed.

Working on my own was not easy. No early morning team huddles, no colleagues to bounce ideas off. No one to whinge to about the boss, or the awful coffee spewed out by the drinks machine. It was just me.

To combat this rather lonely existence I devoured motivational books and listened for hours to audio cassettes. (Hey, it was a long time ago. Ask your mum or dad if you don't know what a cassette was.) One phrase I read became my mantra – 'carpe diem: seize the day.' I actually wrote it in large, bold letters on a piece of white card and stuck it on the wall of my office-cum-bedroom.

Fast forward a few years and I'm still sitting in the same office, at the same desk, with the same bed. But this particular day

I'm feeling like a small child on Christmas morning. I'm reading through an information pack sent to me by an organization that runs public seminars throughout the UK, the US, and Asia. They're looking to recruit some freelance speakers to deliver their seminars. Topics include service excellence, time management, and leadership. I'm loving reading about their approach to business, the opportunities they provide, and the kind of speakers they're looking for.

Then I come to the final page: method of application. *'Please apply by sending a one-hour video of yourself speaking ideally to between 50–100 people. If you don't possess such a video you're probably not ready to join us yet.'*

It's amazing how quickly emotions can fluctuate isn't it? My feelings were similar to finding out I'd got my favourite toy for Christmas and then discovering it wouldn't work as it didn't come with batteries.

You see, at the time I didn't have a five-minute video of me presenting, never mind one hour. I ran small workshops. Average group size? Twelve. I was gutted.

I placed the application pack in the bin. Oh well, it wasn't meant to be, I reasoned to myself. I decided to call my wife in the hope she would be able to offer me some comfort. As I reached for the phone I noticed the words 'carpe diem: seize the day' still stuck on my wall. I looked down at the bin and a thought crossed my mind.

Had I dismissed my chances too quickly?

The reality was I probably hadn't. But something about that quote made me reassess my options. It really was a fantastic opportunity. If I had to write my own dream job specification, this would have come pretty close.

I decided to seize the day.

I removed the information pack from the bin and re-read the final page. On one level nothing had changed. They still wanted a one-hour video of me speaking in front of a large group. But on another level, something had changed. Significantly.

My attitude.

I re-read those same words, but now I was looking for a reason to apply, rather than a reason not to. And I noticed a word I hadn't noticed before. 'Speaking *ideally* in front of a group of 50–100 people.'

I remember thinking, 'Paul, you don't live in an ideal world.'

So, I hired a room and rang all my mates, inviting them to a free one-hour motivational workshop. I bribed them with offers of free food and alcohol.

And having rung all of them, they both said they would come.

I managed to round up some family members, and the numbers soared to a grand total of eight. I ran the session and Helen filmed it on an old camcorder that looked like it had first been used by Adam to film Eve eating apples. (This all happened long before smartphones were available.)

I sent the video tape, along with a covering letter explaining that what they were about to watch was completely contrived, but I genuinely believed I could do the job.

They became my biggest client.

Several years later I was recounting the story at a business breakfast event in London. As people were leaving, a guy approached me and said 'I liked your closing story. I'm going straight back to my office, writing a quote on a piece of paper, and putting it on the wall next to my computer.'

'Carpe Diem?' I enquired.

'No … It's a good quote, but I'm going to write this:

Don't leave your dreams in the bin.'

I guess that might sound a little cheesy to some, but I wonder how often we've thought about an idea, had a particular goal, but then, for a whole host of reasons, binned it?

Great Life Insight

It's so easy to become side-tracked, distracted, or simply overwhelmed by the busyness of life.

Perhaps it wasn't really a dream that you'd binned, but more of a wishful fantasy. Maybe you did start out with positive intentions but due to slow progress or discouragement from others you began to believe it just wasn't meant to be and simply gave up.

Well, whatever the reason, I wonder if now would be a good time to re-examine some of those discarded dreams? You'll find some you were right to bin. Some dreams were merely delusions. And others will remain untouched because perhaps deep down you simply didn't desire them enough.

If that's the case, fine, move on. But what if there is still something nagging inside you?

In the words of Zig Ziglar (great name, don't you think?),

> At the end of your days don't be the kind of person who says, 'I wish I had, I wish I had, I wish I had.' Be the kind of person who says, 'I'm glad I did, I'm glad I did, I'm glad I did.'

That's what Carole did.

Her husband was a biker and he longed for her to join in on some of his weekend adventures. However, she'd developed a mental block about riding a bike, and convinced herself she could never learn. But she heard me tell the story about not leaving your dream in the bin, and as a result she decided to take action. Months later she tweeted me a photo of her and her husband on their bikes.

Not every dream you pursue will have that outcome though.

I dreamt of being a TV presenter. I paid for myself to go on a course on how to become one. I got a showreel. I spoke to people in the industry. It was a dream I'm glad I pursued, but ultimately, I didn't want it enough. The course revealed that perhaps I wouldn't be as fulfilled in that role as I had initially thought. And that's fine. I've no regrets. I'm doing what I love now. But at least I pursued it.

So, what about you?

Success, fulfilment, and happiness do not mysteriously manifest themselves. They come as a result of doing something and being someone.

Great Life Insight

The future isn't a place to get to, it's a place you get to create.

There are no guarantees you'll succeed in what you pursue, but there is a guarantee you'll fail if you never try.

So perhaps the first step is to re-examine some of those discarded dreams and, whatever the ultimate outcome, be able to say … 'I'm glad I did.'

Chapter 12

YOUR PAST IS NOT YOUR PRISON

Have you noticed how certain incidents from your childhood seem permanently tattooed on your memory? Your first kiss. The first song or album you ever bought. A favourite holiday.

I'll never forget my first visit to a football ground. It was to watch Manchester United play at Old Trafford in the early 1970s. George Best played that day. I was in awe of the vastness of the stadium and the noise of the crowd. They're sights and sounds I can still recall vividly today.

I will also never forget what happened to me when I was around nine years old.

I was given a new bike. Not brand new, but that didn't matter. The frame was painted in my favourite colour, orange. I was so excited when I got to sit on it for the first time. And then I was off, cycling down the road where I lived, hesitantly at first, but then with more confidence.

I had not ridden for a few years, but it felt fantastic to do so again. I was so happy, and beamed with pride as I cycled back home.

My step-father saw it differently. He had been watching me and convinced my mum that 'the big fat one', as he referred to me, couldn't ride a bike.

And so I didn't. For several years.

That's just one incident from the years I spent with a psychologically and emotionally abusive step-father.

There are many more.

I won't pretend that his behaviour didn't impact me long after he left my life. It did.

None of us are immune to the effects of our past.

Now don't get me wrong, not all my past experiences were bad. Despite my step-father's intense dislike of me, I can still recall some happy memories from my childhood. But it's the painful ones that can still haunt me on occasions.

Here's the challenge:

Many people, myself included, can hang onto their history and their hurts, and see them as reasons for where they now find themselves in life.

I understand why that happens. I've been there. I've got the T-shirt. But I'm also convinced of this:

Great Life Insight

Scars remind us of where we've been. Not where we're going.

The reality is, our past describes what has happened. It doesn't define what *will* happen. That's a really important truth to hold on to.

Great Life Insight

Your past will always be part of who you are, but it's not the sole factor in who you become.

If you're reading this and you have had a particularly challenging past, please do take time to digest what I'm saying. Our goal is to live a great life, not a perfect one. So, it's important to remember that we can either remain a prisoner of those events and experiences, or recognize that, although they may have impacted us significantly, we don't have to be enslaved by them for the rest of our lives.

Now I appreciate that's not always easy. Perhaps, like me, you may need counselling or some other form of professional support to help you work through your pain, but believe me, it's possible.

Great Life Insight

Maybe it's time to realize our past is not a life sentence, it's a life lesson.

Those lessons learnt can help not only you but perhaps others too. And how you've overcome your challenges can be an inspiration to others.

So, I didn't get to ride a bike for several years, and throughout my school years I was mocked and sometimes even humiliated about my weight.

But do you know the irony of all this now, over 40 years later? My business brand is 'The SUMO Guy'. And my logo? It's of a rather large guy on a unicycle!

Before I finish, take a moment not just to read the following words from the author James R. Sherman, but to meditate on them. Write them down. Commit them to memory. I hope they inspire you as much as they do me.

You can't go back and create a new beginning –
but you can start now and create a new ending.

Powerful, eh?

Words can change worlds can't they?

So, remember this:

Don't dwell on the past.

There's no future in it.

Perhaps it's now time to leave the prison of your past and embrace and enjoy the freedom of your future.

Chapter 13

STRUGGLES CAN STRENGTHEN YOU

Μy Aussie mate Steve is an amazing guy. As I write he's two-thirds of the way through an epic journey riding around various parts of the world on his motorbike. He's already ridden across Australia, the US, Korea, Russia (he started in Siberia), and parts of Europe. The final part of his journey will be across Africa, and he's doing it all to raise money and awareness for the charity Water Aid.

We managed to catch up whilst he was having a stop off in London (sadly his epic tour didn't involve taking in the delights of my home town, Warrington).

As we chatted, I suddenly realized how boring it would have been if, when we talked about his trip, he replied 'Everything has been great. The weather has been wonderful. The logistics have been spot on. I've had no mechanical problems, and I've met some wonderful people. Despite spending weeks on my own I have enjoyed every moment of my own company and ridden with a permanent grin on my face as I realized how lucky I am to do what I do.'

If that was Steve's reply I would have been pleased for him on one level, but, if I'm honest, disappointed on another.

I've got a feeling Steve would too.

You see, there would have been no 'war stories' to talk about. There would have been little to engage his listener when he was sharing his story because there had been no challenges to overcome (apart from the challenge of riding all those miles, obviously).

In the words of my kids when they were growing up, the trip would have been 'easy peasy lemon squeezy'.

As it happens, that wasn't Steve's experience.

There were times of struggle.

The solitude got to him on occasions. The weather in the US was unexpectedly poor. Russian drivers seemed keen to cut short his journey and probably also his life, and he met some 'interesting' guys in Siberia who appeared intent on stealing his bike.

Added to that, he also had a run-in with the police in South Korea and still had the logistical challenge of getting his bike shipped to Tanzania.

Trust me, it was fascinating to hear Steve recount his stories and talk about his struggles.

Here's the deal:

A great life, one that is filled with success, fulfilment, and happiness, will also include some struggles.

Great Life Insight

It's often when we've faced and overcome challenges that we feel most fulfilled.

Put quite simply – no struggle, no story.

In reality, we don't always want life to be 'easy peasy lemon squeezy'.

It's nice some of the time, but not all the time.

Life will become incredibly boring and unfulfilling without some struggles along the way.

It's the struggle that makes you.

If you play a sport, how do you improve? By always playing against players you know you can beat, or those who are better than you?

In life it's the people who struggle, often despite setbacks, who achieve success and who we admire. They realize that nothing great is ever really achieved without some struggle.

Now those struggles can come in various guises: sometimes it's overcoming self-doubt, ill-health, broken relationships, financial problems, negative publicity, uncertain times. The list can go on and on.

Believe me, I know what I'm talking about.

2015 was an incredibly challenging time in my life personally. There were occasions when emotionally I felt close to breaking point. When I got together with a few speaker friends at the end of the year, we shared our biggest achievements from the previous 12 months. Some talked about having a record year financially. One talked about signing a new book deal. My achievement was simply this: 'Holding it together when inside I was falling apart.'

That year has helped shape me. It's made me better equipped for other challenges. It's made me realize that if I can get through that, I can get through most things.

And here's what's interesting:

As a result, I'm more compassionate about other people's struggles.

Great Life Insight

Recognize that behind someone's glory there's inevitably a story.

You see, rarely do people glide to success – they've usually had to grunt their way there.

I admit some struggles are born out of stupidity, poor planning, and reckless decision-making. But some arise purely and simply as a consequence of doing life and wanting to make a difference.

Even in the midst of them, remember a great life can still be experienced.

What you go through, you can grow through.

Your struggles can strengthen you … if you allow them to.

Chapter 14

HAVE THE COURAGE TO QUIT ... SOMETIMES

I've a lot of admiration for my mate Dave. Several years ago, he gained a Guinness record for memorizing Pi to 22,500 digits. He trained for over six months. Recalling all those digits took over four hours (imagine being the adjudicator for that one). But here's what's interesting (although I don't think that's quite the word Dave would have used) – after initially recalling 18,000 digits he got one wrong. Bummer, eh?

So, he had a choice: quit and miss out on the record or come back the next day and start all over again.

He came back the next day, failed a further three times, changed his strategy, and eventually claimed the record.

Dave, along with countless other people, had refused to quit in the face of a setback. It's an admirable trait to have, and one we're encouraged to adopt if we want to achieve success. In fact, you may be familiar with the motivational quote '*A winner never quits and a quitter never wins.*' I guess that sounds like a wonderful mantra to have – and it can be. Sometimes.

But in certain circumstances I think it's downright stupid.

Let me explain.

My friend Steve wanted to climb Mount Kilimanjaro. His enthusiasm for the adventure was infectious, to the point that I initially thought I might do it with him. He organized weekend hikes, did all the research, and read, it seemed, every book there was on the subject. Having decided my dodgy knees might just about cope climbing the mountain but might struggle coming down it, I declined the opportunity to join the group.

A few weeks before the climb I bumped into Steve and asked how long before he embarked on his adventure. He took out his phone and proudly announced '16 days, 4 hours, and 19 minutes'. He had a countdown clock synced to his phone.

But Steve never completed the climb he was so desperate to do.

Having spoken about nothing else for over a year, he was affected by altitude sickness and had to turn back. He could have tried to carry on, but in doing so he would have risked his own safety, and possibly even his life. It was a hard but wise decision to quit. I admire him for it.

I also admire my son's mate, who chose to leave his university course. It just wasn't for him. Why persist with something you clearly don't enjoy?

Yet the pressure is often on us to persevere, isn't it? I understand why, but sometimes it's not the right advice, and for our own long-term happiness (despite the short-term pain it may cause) quitting can be the best thing to do.

As Dan and Chip Heath write in their book *Decisive – How to Make Better Choices in Life and Work,* 'at some point the virtue of being persistent turns into the vice of denying reality.'

But our society tends to celebrate people like my friend Dave who refuse to quit and hold steadfast to their dreams. Steve, on the other hand, is rarely asked to talk about his decision to quit trying to climb Kilimanjaro.

But guess what?

Research quoted in the *Harvard Business Review* shows that people can waste enormous amounts of time and energy persisting with unrealistic goals, a phenomenon known as 'false hope syndrome'.

And here's something else:

Having too much resilience can, in fact, result in people tolerating too much adversity, demoralizing work, or bad bosses for longer than is healthy.

Great Life Insight

Saying 'I've had enough' or 'I'm out of here' could be incredibly liberating rather than a sign of defeat.

Now this might not sound like a typical message coming from someone known as a motivational speaker, but is there any harm in knowing your limits and having realistic expectations? Such an attitude meant I didn't even attempt to climb Kilimanjaro, and Steve is not talked about as some hero who refused to give up on his dream but lost his life in the process.

And here's a key reason why having the courage to quit sometimes can actually help you achieve a great life. You see, strategic quitting (in other words, planned and thought through) frees you up to focus on your real priorities in life.

Great Life Insight

By stopping something or saying no, you free yourself up to say yes to something better.

Who knows what you may go on to enjoy and achieve when you do so?

Here's the deal:

Have the courage to admit when things are not working. Have the courage to admit you're travelling on a path that might please others but doesn't fulfil you. Have the courage to be the best version of you that you can be, rather than feel you have to emulate others.

Now of course there are consequences to quitting. Don't act rashly. Seek advice from a range of people and think through your next steps carefully. Make sure you're strategic rather than reactive in your decision-making.

Let me be really clear about my message here.

To have a great life we need to show resilience in the face of setbacks. And there is plenty to be gained by refusing to quit and persevering. Believe me, they're great qualities to have.

But equally, so is having the courage to quit sometimes. Not only does it take guts, but it can free you up to focus on what you really need to do to have a great life. The reality is that sometimes the end is not the end. It can be the doorway to a new beginning.

So, Dave and Steve. Two different stories. Two different approaches. Two different outcomes.

But both are still happy.

The 'one size fits all' approach to life doesn't work – you see, sometimes winners know when to quit and quitters go on to win.

And you can quote me on that.

Chapter 15

WALLOWING IS OK ... FOR A WHILE

I was so excited. It was the equivalent of hearing that Bradford City and Wigan Athletic had both won on the same day. A national newspaper was going to serialize my latest book. This wasn't going to be a brief mention – this was daily, double-page spread coverage for a week.

My book was on the subject of worry, and although hugely satisfied with what I'd written, I was ironically a little concerned as to how it would do in comparison to my other books.

Well, now I could relax. It seemed success was guaranteed.

My publisher was equally excited. A serialization of a book in this genre was usually reserved for self-help gurus like Paul McKenna. Now it seemed it was Paul McGee's turn. Such coverage of the book, I was assured, would bring bestseller status.

I was on cloud ten (cloud nine was full of other people). On one level, life would go on as before, but my publisher was convinced that as 'worry' was such a hot topic my profile would be raised to such an extent that other sections of the media, including television, would also seek me out. I tried to play it low key to the rest of my team, but inside I was thrilled. I celebrated that night with a vanilla slice and a pale ale and watched Bradford play Crewe with my mate Dave.

I know how to party.

But then something happened. Or perhaps more accurately, didn't happen.

The newspaper changed its mind.

The book was never serialized. There was no negotiation. No second chance. Paul McKenna could sleep easy at night.

I was totally gutted. More so than by Bradford's 1–0 defeat at Crewe.

And here's what's really interesting: I'm known for the phrase SUMO – Shut Up, Move On. I guess that's what I should have advised myself to do, but you know what? At that moment in time, I wasn't ready to.

What did I want to do instead?

Have a right good wallow.

Great Life Insight

It's not always easy to dismiss a setback. We're not always ready to immediately move on.

The reality is we're humans after all, not machines. Of course, you can put on your happy face and pretend everything is fine, but there are times (not every time I admit) when to do so would be both unrealistic and quite frankly unhealthy.

Great Life Insight

A great life is not one devoid of disappointment. Happiness is not the absence of things going wrong.

But sometimes we're encouraged to deny our disappointment and our feelings of sadness, aren't we?

Well, I've some advice for you. Don't.

Hey, if you need to sit with your sadness, do so. If you need to vent about missing out on promotion or your dream job, do so. If you need to cry about that broken relationship, do so.

It's OK to wallow for a while. It's OK to not always feel OK.

Great Life Tip

> Don't paper over your pain. Sometimes you need to express it, not suppress it.

Now of course we need to get perspective here. I'm not suggesting we hold a large pity party due to a missed train, a spot on your nose, or because your team failed to beat Crewe.

What I am saying is this: there are occasions when it's healthy and necessary to acknowledge, accept, and process the emotions we're experiencing.

The world will continue to turn, and life will continue to go on, but you may just need some time and space to wallow.

However, this next point is crucial.

Recognize that how you're feeling now is valid but remember it's also temporary.

The feelings you're experiencing are part of your journey – but they're not your destination.

Wallowing is OK – but it's not meant to be a way of life. If it is, you'll never experience a great life.

My book *How Not to Worry* came out in April 2012. There was no media fanfare. Sales were good, but not spectacular. Friends said it was one of the best books I'd written.

And I did wallow.

For a while.

But then it was time to move on.

Just like it is for all of us.

Chapter 16

NOT ALL WORRIES ARE WORTHLESS

I love working in Australia. I'm proud to say I come from Manchester, and I guess the North West of England will always be my home, but the land down under just shades it on the beaches and its climate. Their coffee isn't bad either.

One phrase I hear a lot when I'm there is 'No worries.'

It doesn't seem to matter what the request is.

'Can I order a taxi?'

'No worries.'

'Can I have my eggs poached?'

'No worries.'

'Can you amputate my arm with a knife and fork?'

'No worries.'

I love it in many ways. However, the reality is we do worry. A lot. Even the Aussies do, despite their favourite catchphrase. And clearly, doing so can ultimately rob us of a great life.

The subject of worry has fascinated me for years. So much so I even wrote a book on the topic. You see, I'm curious as to why we worry, particularly when you think about the following.

If you're reading this book and living in what is often described as the developed free world then let me ask you three questions:

How does it feel to be one of the wealthiest people ever to have lived on this planet?

How does it feel to know your life expectancy is higher than any other generation that's ever been born?

How does it feel to have the opportunity to travel and discover more of life's riches in a week than most people previously had in a lifetime?

The reality is, in a generation where an overwhelming sense of gratitude should be our defining emotion, it seems fear and worry in all their guises are actually more pervasive.

Now, given that, you would probably expect me to jump on the rather crowded bandwagon packed with purveyors of positivity and tell you it's wrong to worry, be more grateful, and get on with it.

Hey, if only it was that easy, right? Well, sorry to disappoint you, but I gave up my ticket for that ride some time ago.

Whilst I admit incessant worrying can have a seriously damaging impact on both your state of mind and your physical health, I think there are times when a small amount of short-term worrying might actually be helpful.

I refer to this approach as 'worth it worry'.

Let me explain.

When the primitive part of your brain perceives a threat, it releases the hormones adrenaline, noradrenaline, and cortisol. This immediately stimulates and energizes you. Your body is preparing you for a potential challenge.

Now of course the perceived threat could actually be something quite trivial and even imaginary. However, your brain isn't taking any chances. You're now on high alert and sometimes this can be really helpful.

Why?

Because it can potentially spur us on towards positive, constructive action.

Here's an example.

I was recently going on holiday to Lisbon (worth checking out if you've never been) with my family and we were booked onto an early morning flight. Now I love early morning flights – you arrive at the airport at some unearthly hour and have time to observe hundreds of people eating a full English breakfast and washing it down with a few pints of beer.

And that's just the cabin crew.

I was working in Glasgow the day before our holiday and, although we were flying from Manchester, I would have plenty of time to get home and pack the night before.

Or so I thought.

It was only after a briefing call with my client that I realized they were wanting me to give a pre-dinner talk that was due to finish at around 7:30 p.m.

I then discovered the event was not actually taking place in Glasgow but in a location 20 miles outside the city.

My last train home was at 8:10 p.m.

I had approximately 40 minutes to get to the station after my talk. That was doable, but it was cutting it a bit fine.

I guess my Aussie mates would have said 'no worries' and some well-meaning self-help guru would have told me to put my trust in the universe and everything would work out just perfectly.

I was less convinced. In fact, I was worried.

Not in an irrational or hysterical way, but with a real concern that if the logistics didn't work out, then my family might be getting that early flight to Lisbon without me.

But here's the thing: those worries prompted me to take action.

Rather than be locked into a cycle of '"what if?" worry' I simply decided to ask myself how I could influence or improve the situation. I couldn't affect the time of the train's departure, but perhaps I could affect the start and finish time of my talk.

So, I managed to negotiate with my client the same length of talk but starting 15 minutes earlier. Not only that, but I explored alternative trains home from other stations in Scotland if I missed mine.

I relaxed.

My worries were worth it.

They provoked me to take action and conduct something called a 'pre-mortem'.

Great Life Tip

Conduct a pre-mortem where you anticipate what things could go wrong before the event and take the necessary steps to prevent them happening.

Some might call this pessimistic. I call it being prepared.

Because of '"worth it" worry' and the pre-mortem approach, I was able to channel my energies solely into my work, rather than panicking about missing my train home.

Now please hear me right. Worry can disable you and rob you of your happiness. I'm certainly not encouraging you to do more of it. But ...

Great Life Insight

Don't always resist your worries. Perhaps they're flagging up issues that, with planning and preparation, you could resolve.

The reality is, some worries are definitely worthless because there is nothing you can do to influence or improve the situation. But sometimes they could be worth it.

Make that distinction and you've just helped yourself live a calmer and ultimately happier life.

My talk went well, and I caught the train home in time. I celebrated the next day with the classic combination of a bacon butty and a beer at the airport – because, just like worry, sometimes I'm worth it.

Chapter 17

DETHRONE THE DRAMA QUEEN

I have a confession. When I'm travelling by train I have a tendency to eavesdrop on other people's conversations. Admittedly, some people are talking so loudly that it's hard not to, especially if they're speaking on the phone to someone.

On some occasions I've even been known to ask my wife to speak more quietly during a meal at a restaurant whilst I tune into the juicy conversation at the next table – especially if it looks like it's going to develop into a row.

My natural curiosity gets the best of me I'm afraid, and, to be fair, my wife can become equally engrossed in the conversation unfolding nearby.

Now please tell me we're not the only ones who've ever done that!

During these moments of eavesdropping I'm often intrigued by the language people use to describe day-to-day events.

Ever heard any of these?

'It's been a total nightmare.'

'I've had the day from hell.'

'I can't stand this anymore.'

My guess is that, if you have, it's not necessarily due to the fact that you were delivering foreign aid to a war-torn country or visiting a refugee camp. If you're like me, you hear these kinds of phrases just going about your everyday business.

And if you're like me, you've probably used them yourself.

It does seem that many of us have developed quite a taste for the melodramatic doesn't it? We like a bit of drama after all, and it's a nice way to spice up what, at times, may be a rather mundane Monday.

Some of us may even have mates who love to help drum up a drama and rev up our emotions. I sometimes refer to them as 'escalators' – the kind of people who love to escalate an issue, highlighting how awful things are and urging us to feel more angry and upset about things than we originally were.

If you're not convinced such people exist, then just check out some of the comments sections on social media. Actually, on second thoughts don't – you've probably got enough challenges in your life as it is.

So, is all this self-induced drama doing any harm?

Well, if it happens very occasionally then probably not.

But what if it's happening on a regular or even a daily basis? In that case you might be adding a little too much spice to your life and overheating as a result.

Let me explain.

Creating mountains out of molehills can make us lose perspective. Our internal and external conversations can add fuel to our anxiety and in doing so escalate our worries.

In such cases, life can become a battle to be fought rather than an experience to be enjoyed.

Great Life Insight

Our framing of situations and the ways in which we talk about them can actually disempower us and weaken our ability to tackle them.

Perhaps that's how we want to live life. Seeing ourselves as the powerless victim, constantly struggling against the daily tribulations that life has to throw at us.

But such an attitude is not helping you create a great life.

Missing your train is frustrating, but it's not the end of the world.

Your friends forgetting your birthday is not a major calamity.

And your kid's new tattoo? Hey, they're five years old, they need to make their own choices in life.

So here are three really important things to remind yourself of:

- **Problems are not permanent.** Remember the phrase 'This too will pass.'

- **Problems are not pervasive.** Just because things are going wrong in one area of your life doesn't mean they're going wrong in every area of your life.

- **Problems are not personal.** It's easy to think you're the only person who has ever encountered this particular event or issue before. Believe me, you're not.

I'm not suggesting you deny or suppress your feelings. Just be careful you don't exaggerate how awful the situation is and lose perspective.

Trust me, that is not a recipe for resilience.

Great Life Insight

When we magnify our misfortunes we move from understandable sadness to unhelpful self-pity.

Yes, I realize there are days from hell and nightmare scenarios, but thankfully for most of us these are rare.

So, if you want to feel a little bit happier about life, dethrone the drama queen.

Oh, and if you are going to have a row in a restaurant, just check out who's at the table next to you. And don't forget to wave.

Chapter 18

GET THINGS IN PERSPECTIVE

'So, can I just confirm that neither you nor any of your neighbours are on the phone?'

'That's correct' I replied.

'OK then, but if something does go wrong during your wife's operation, if there's a life or death situation, then we'll send a policeman round', the nurse said, rather unreassuringly.

This was the late 1980s. A time when the media were obsessed with Princess Diana's latest outfit and mobile phones were as rare as a hot summer's day in Manchester.

My wife Helen had been rushed into hospital with appendicitis. There was a concern that her appendix might burst, something the medical staff assured me was not particularly pleasant and could be dangerous. As next of kin, I was the person they would need to contact if something went wrong.

They had no reason to believe it would – however, covering all their bases and addressing the issue of how to contact me when I wasn't on the phone (we were living in a small rented flat at the time), a policeman would be sent round to me.

I left Helen as she was being taken to the operating theatre, squeezing her hand and reassuring her I wouldn't steal any of her chocolate whilst she was under the anaesthetic.

It was late. I was tired, and I crashed out immediately on my return to our flat.

I slept peacefully.

Until 3 a.m., when I woke to the sound of a doorbell ringing. I turned to Helen.

She wasn't there.

My mind quickly kicked into gear. Of course, I was alone. I'd left Helen at the hospital.

The doorbell rang again.

Who on earth was wanting to see me at 3 o'clock in the morning?

Then I remembered:

> 'If there's a life or death situation, we'll send a policeman round.'

I leapt out of bed and grabbed a dressing gown to cover my modesty and my Bradford City boxer shorts.

My mind went into overdrive.

It was a simple operation.

She was in good hands.

We'd only been married just over a year (as if that made any difference).

I convinced myself it was probably just some drunk passing by trying to cause a disturbance.

But the doorbell then rang a third time. If it was a drunk they were certainly persistent.

I moved quickly towards the door – and under my breath I muttered to myself, 'Please don't be a policeman.'

I opened the door.

A policeman stood before me.

'I'm looking for a Mr McGee.'

'You've found him', I replied.

'Mr McGee, I've got some bad news. Do you mind if I come in?'

I was stunned. For a moment I just stared at him, unable to say or do anything.

Finally, I said 'You'd better come in.'

I walked hesitantly back towards our small lounge – my mind continuing to process the events unfolding before me.

My wife was dead? Really?

The policeman followed and as I sat down I broke my silence.

'It's about Helen, isn't it?'

'Who?' asked the slightly bemused officer.

'Helen, my wife. They said at the hospital…'

'Sir,' interrupted the policeman, 'I'm not sure what you're on about. But do you own a Peugeot 104?'

'Er… yes', I replied with a face that did little to hide my confusion.

'Well, I'm sorry sir but I've some bad news. It's been stolen and left abandoned around ten miles away from here. I'm afraid to say it's been trashed. It would seem someone's stood on the bonnet and kicked in your front windscreen. It's a real mess.'

'Really?' I replied with a face that had moved from one of confusion to borderline ecstasy.

The policeman looked completely bemused.

'Sir, did you know your car had been stolen? Because your response does seem rather unusual.'

So, I got off his lap.

It was time to bring him up to speed.

'Sorry officer, I thought you'd come to tell me my wife was dead. But actually you're just here to tell me my car's been stolen.'

The above is a story from nearly 30 years ago. It's a reminder that it's important to get perspective. And I would like to be able to say the lessons learnt have stayed with me ever since.

Sadly, they haven't always.

To be fair, our biology doesn't help us.

Our primitive emotional brain has evolved to act first, think later. It's instinctive, reactive, and impulsive.

It's difficult for the rational part of our brain to get a look-in sometimes.

That's why today I still stress at times over stupid things.

I can, like most of us, get caught up in the minutiae of life and lose sight of what's really important.

But I'm getting better.

I'm taking control of my thoughts, my internal dialogue.

Great Life Tip

> Refuse to allow your thoughts to run wild and turn the trivial into something terrible.

Of course, not everything is trivial, but I'm now more aware of the impact of the primitive emotional part of my brain and I'm learning to engage my rational brain more often.

How do I do that?

One way is to ask myself a simple question.

'Where is this issue on a scale of 1–10? (Where 10 = death).'

I use that question regularly and here's what I've realized.

You know what? The state of my daughter's bedroom is no longer a nine.

My reaction to the person who I let into the traffic while driving – and who didn't thank me – is not an eight.

Here's the deal: to live a happier life, it's crucial we get a sense of perspective and avoid overreacting to situations. That's easy to say, but it's becoming increasingly hard to do. Why? The pace at which many of us now seem to live our lives.

Great Life Insight

Frantic and full lives lived out continually in the fast lane can undermine our sense of wellbeing.

The buzz we get from living this way will ultimately be our downfall.

We'll overreact, make stupid decisions, and damage relationships.

Above all, we'll be harming ourselves.

So, we need to take control, step back, and get perspective.

Psychologists call it 'cognitive reappraisal'. I like the term 'frame it to tame it'.

As a result, I'm learning to see problems for what they are. They're rarely, if ever, life or death situations. They're a pain, they're frustrating, and I wish they wouldn't happen – but they're not life threatening.

Two of my closest friends in the speaking business are no longer with us. Clive and Kenny both passed away in their early fifties. When I'm defrosting my windscreen on a bitterly cold, dark January morning after a night's stay in a Premier Inn on an industrial estate near Dudley, I think about them. I often think 'You know what Paul, Clive and Kenny would love to swap places with you now.'

It helps me get perspective.

Yes, life will throw up some high scores sometimes. And none of us will escape the occasional ten. But life isn't filled entirely with high scores.

So, calm down and put things into perspective.

By the way, the car got repaired, Helen's operation was a success, but the policeman was still confused.

Oh, and I didn't steal Helen's chocolate – it would have been a ten if I had.

Chapter 19

NEVER UNDERESTIMATE THE POWER OF PAUSE

When I was growing up the technology associated with television was a bit different to today. OK, that's underplaying things a little – it was vastly different. For a start, we didn't have colour television, everything was in black and white, and programmes were only shown during limited times of the day. One of the stations (to be fair we only had three) used to end its broadcasting schedule with the playing of the national anthem.

And when we wanted to change channels we had to push or twiddle the knobs on the television. There were no remote controls. And that had its benefits. Firstly, no single member of the family could hog the remote, and secondly you didn't spend half an hour lifting cushions, looking under the cat, or running round the house asking 'Has anyone seen the remote?'

The lack of a remote control also made the nation fitter, particularly if you enjoyed channel surfing (across all three of them) as you physically had to keep moving up and down and walking to and from the television. Even those with a small living room with a television almost within touching distance of the sofa at least got to do some stretching exercises – you didn't need yoga or Pilates in those days.

One other technological challenge I faced when growing up was that if you missed your favourite TV show, that was it. We didn't even have the facilities to record programmes until I was in my teenage years. Tough life, eh?

So, you can see that I'm not looking back nostalgically and thinking 'they were the good old days'. No way. I love the fact that you can now record programmes, watch catch-up TV, fast-forward through adverts, watch in high definition, and also pause the programme you're watching. I love the power of being able to freeze the action, to momentarily stop a story unfolding, or to draw out the tension during a football penalty shootout (unless I'm watching England, in which case I fast forward to the bit where you see their opponents celebrating). The power of the pause button gives me the opportunity to catch my breath, to get myself a drink, or to have a comfort break.

It's great that you can do that with television, but it's not always so easy to do with life, is it? To press pause. To take time out. To catch your breath.

It's not easy, but neither is it impossible.

The problem is, most of us are often living life on fast-forward – busy, rushing, doing. We're fighting fires, reacting to emails, multi-tasking, texting, tweeting, and twerking. (OK, maybe not that last one, but I couldn't resist including it.) And before we know it another day has gone. Another day lived on fast-forward.

But guess what?

Great Life Insight

You have the remote control to your own life.

Sadly, it doesn't come with a rewind button, but if you look carefully you'll notice it does give you the option to press pause. And believe me, you need to use it.

You see, in a world of 24/7 news and instant access to anything and everything, it's easy to spend our lives overwhelmed with information and constantly reacting to situations.

It's easy to live life this way.

But no one said it was compulsory.

Great Life Insight

'There is more to life than increasing its speed.'—Gandhi

Pressing pause means taking a minute, or even just a moment, to reflect. It means taking time to process what you're reading and learning rather than instantly judging or replying.

It means going outside, taking a walk, and giving your brain a break. It means time out for you. It means you can, even in the midst of the whirlwind, find some moments of peace.

But only if you make them.

Pressing pause gives you a chance to reflect and ask yourself some questions. Ones I often ask myself include:

> 'How did I handle that situation?'
>
> 'What did I enjoy about today?'
>
> 'What did I learn today?'
>
> 'Did I take time out for me today?'
>
> 'I wonder what's going on in that person's world right now?'

The reality is, we will still react at times. And the busyness and pace of life will mean we'll feel we've fast-forwarded through certain days. I get that.

But that doesn't have to be every day. Not if you want to live a great life.

So, take time to practise the pause.

When in doubt, pause.

When tired, pause.

When stressed, pause.

When enjoying a beautiful moment, pause.

You see, the pause can determine the quality of your life. And you've got the remote.

So, use it.

Chapter 20

HANG OUT WITH HUMILITY

At a seminar I presented recently I asked around a hundred business people what they considered to be an essential character trait for achieving success. They came up with over 20 different ones. Humility didn't make anyone's list.

Passion, drive, courage, determination, and vision all featured high on the list and I agree they're all key elements to success, but I think most people underestimate the crucial role humility can play.

Why's it such a big deal? You're about to find out.

Now let me clarify. I'm a big believer in backing yourself. I'm convinced a lack of self-belief can rob people of reaching their potential, but as I've got older and a little wiser I've also come to realize that a lack of humility can actually derail you. And, interestingly, we're probably most prone to lacking humility when we've had some success. When this happens, we can feel 'we've arrived'. But we need to be careful, because if our success is not managed well it can lead to arrogance and complacency, which are both breeding grounds for failure.

So why is humility not seen as important? I think it's because we can see being humble as a weakness and not a sign of strength. However, I love the quote by author and pastor Rick Warren on this subject:

Great Life Insight

'Humility is not thinking less about yourself, it's thinking about yourself less.'

For me, humility is not a question of putting yourself down, it's simply a recognition that the world doesn't revolve solely around you.

In my experience, one of the most important traits of humility that counters the onset of arrogance and complacency is the willingness to be open to new ideas and a desire for life-long learning. Here's a brilliant example of that.

Michelangelo, the Italian sculptor, painter, architect, and poet (see what you could get done before social media arrived?) said, when aged 87, 'I am still learning.'

I love that, don't you?

He was considered to be the greatest living artist of his time, but clearly Michelangelo didn't feel such an honour made him exempt from continuing his learning journey.

In my own life I'm challenged by the words of Daniel Boorstin, the American historian. Take a moment to reflect on them:

Great Life Insight

'Our greatest obstacle to learning is not ignorance. It is the illusion of knowledge.'

Ouch. That's one I need to take on board, and why I consider being called an expert a potentially dangerous thing. Why? Well, plenty of people are known as experts, but embracing humility is a reminder that we need to continue our learning and be open to new ideas from others. It also means being prepared to have your ideas challenged, to admit you may be wrong about certain things, and to confess that at times your answer to a particular question might be 'I don't know.'

I recognize such an attitude can be a challenge. You see, we like placing other people on pedestals. We love to hero worship. It seems to be part of our DNA. And when you're on the receiving end of that hero worship, it's tempting to believe all the hype. It's easy to be convinced of your own invincibility – to take all the credit for your success and to forget the support you got from others.

So here are two behaviours that will enhance your life, keep you humble, and prevent arrogance and complacency from leading you down a potentially dangerous road.

- **Always be a student.** Your education didn't finish when you left school or college. No matter how qualified you are, continue to be open to learning.

Great Life Insight

Whatever your job title or role in life, remember you're also a full-time student.

Learning can take place anytime, anywhere, and from anyone. It can come from reading a book, listening to a podcast, attending a seminar, or watching something online. But it can also happen through your conversations – and those conversations can happen with colleagues, customers, children, family, and even strangers. Who's to know what you might discover today, and from what unexpected source? So, stay curious – you could be surprised at what you learn.

• **Seek support.** Part of my work involves working with elite sportspeople, mainly from the world of football. One club I worked with was keen for me to get alongside one of its players whose off-the-field problems were affecting his on-field performances. Sadly, he chose not to accept my support, or that of anyone else.

He's no longer at the club.

When I asked why he wouldn't see me, I was told he thought asking for help was a sign of weakness. Trust me, having worked with thousands of people across the world, in a variety of contexts, I'm convinced of the following:

Great Life Insight

Seeking support is never a sign of weakness. It's a sign of wisdom.

Here's the deal: you have the potential to achieve more and be more if only you have the humility to ask for help. And asking for help doesn't necessarily mean you're struggling. It's simply an indication of your desire to get better.

Now that support can come in many guises. In my work I've been a listening ear, an encourager, a sports psychologist, and also a challenger. So, it's important to identify what support you need and from whom.

And because of the help I give others, I'm very conscious of the support I also need. I know I can be vulnerable to burnout, and I'm also hugely aware that although I might be 'the face' of my business, without the work of my team I would be nowhere.

So, remember: those that support others need support themselves.

So, what about you? When did you last seek support or ask for some help?

A whole range of traits make up the qualities required to create a great life. Many of them are obvious, but others perhaps less so. Humility might not be the main quality we hear being talked about in the context of success, but if you want to achieve and maintain it, make sure you don't ignore it. Confidence and self-belief are crucial, just remember humility is there to complement not contradict them.

So, make sure you take time to hang out with it.

Chapter 21

HOW TO AVOID BURNOUT AND A BREAK-UP

2 4 December 1997. Christmas Eve, and my two young children had finally been persuaded to go to bed with the threat that Father Christmas wouldn't visit if they were still awake – or even worse, I would start singing to them.

Whilst I struggled to light the fire in our living room, my wife microwaved our Chinese ready meals and dug out the chopsticks. We always go to a lot of trouble for our romantic meals by the fire.

With the kids tucked up in bed and the fire roaring (I had to rely on fire lighters rather than skill), we settled down to the finest ready meal the Co-op had to offer. We had even splashed out on a portion of prawn crackers and seaweed – it was Christmas after all.

Helen and I seemed to have had less time together since the kids were born, so I relished the opportunity for food, wine, and conversation.

It had been a busy year, business had been good and included lots of travel. Apart from working in Asia I had also had the opportunity to fulfil a lifetime ambition and visit a friend in Australia.

I waxed lyrical as I reminisced about the amazing year we'd had.

Helen, on the other hand, seemed strangely quiet.

Then she finally broke her silence.

'I don't think it's been a good year at all Paul. As a family we rarely see you, and when you are around you always seem stressed. We've had a few days' family holiday on the

Isle of Wight, but you never once seemed to relax when we were there.

I'm glad business is good and that you enjoyed your foreign travels – on your own – but I think next year needs to be very different for us as a family. As far as I'm concerned you seem to have forgotten us and become obsessed with work.'

Her words carried more of a kick than the hot chili beef I was eating.

I could see that my wife of 10 years was clearly upset. We both quickly lost interest in what we were eating and focused instead on some straight talking.

There was a long conversation that night.

A few home truths were spoken, and over the coming weeks I did a lot of soul searching about my priorities in life. I recognized that I did seem to be living in a state of constant stress, and I knew I was far from excelling as a husband or as a father.

Things needed to change.

But how?

Work/life balance seemed both unrealistic and unattainable. I was trying to get a business established and my work involved travelling away from home a significant amount. I loved my work, I felt I was good at it, and after three years on invalidity benefit (I had been ill with M.E., also known as chronic fatigue syndrome) it felt immensely satisfying to be bringing in a reasonable income.

It was time to talk to my closest friend and mentor, Paul.

After a lot of listening to my situation, Paul's first advice to me was to think about the term 'blend' rather than balance in relation to my life. He suggested that trying to balance all aspects of your life was an unhelpful way to view things.

But blend was different.

Paul elaborated further.

A smoothie or a juice is made up of different ingredients blended together – and here's the key point: each ingredient is important, but you don't necessarily have equal amounts of each in the drink.

Paul said it's the same with life.

Each aspect of your life is important, but you don't necessarily spend equal amounts of time on each of them. However, life, just like the drink, doesn't taste so good without all of the ingredients.

He helped me to develop the simple model below to help me enjoy a more blended life.

Together we identified four key areas that I always needed to be mindful of if I was to avoid the sort of predicament I'd found myself in that Christmas Eve.

Over 20 years later, I'm convinced they're crucial for everyone. They were as shown in Figure 21.1.

The model seemed so simple but made so much sense.

It brought me a sense of both clarity and control.

Up until that point I had been focusing purely on my career and finances. I wasn't wrong to focus on them, but

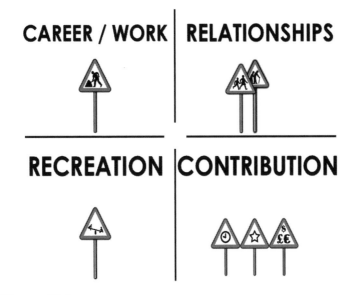

Figure 21.1

I was ignoring the other three areas. Paul encouraged me to prioritize time in building my relationship with Helen and my kids, Matt and Ruth.

This meant planning time to be together, making sure I spoke to them every day when I was away, and realizing how crucial it was to be more conscious of what we did together, rather than give them the dregs of my energy when work was over.

His challenge was that it was great to look for new ways to promote my business, but how about applying the same kind of thinking to my relationships and be more proactive in seeking ways to improve them?

It wasn't about trying to spend as much time with my family as I did at work – that wasn't realistic. It was more about what we did when we were together.

Great Life Insight

What's the point of being popular with your customers and colleagues but a worn-out stranger with your family?

The same applied to my recreation time. What was I doing to recharge and reenergize myself?

Paul's mantra was simple:

Don't leave it to chance, make it a choice.

That meant taking a more holistic view of my health – not just to focus on my physical health (weight and general fitness) but also my mental, spiritual, and emotional health. He encouraged me to take more walks, to read books for pleasure rather than ones simply related to work, and to take more time to reflect.

Finally, he emphasized the importance of not only thinking about my own needs, but also focusing on supporting others – a term he labelled contribution.

I was encouraged to see these not as four separate and distinct areas of my life, but four dimensions that interconnected with each other and helped me to live a more blended life.

That meant that going for long walks with my wife was investing in both my recreation and my relationships. The same was true when going to the football with Matt, or when I had a special dad and daughter weekend in London with Ruth.

Likewise, my work was also contributing to the welfare of others – but I could also use some of my company's profits to make a financial gift to some charities and charge a charity rate for my public seminars.

Great Life Insight

It's hard to live a great life when you're focusing solely on one dimension and have lost sight of the bigger picture.

Here's the deal:

I had genuinely convinced myself that 1997 was a great year. Well, if my definition of 'great' was solely about work and some time for me, then indeed it had been.

But the sacrifice I was making for this so-called success was burnout and a potential broken relationship with those closest to me.

What about you? Which areas of your life do you need to give more attention to? You might want to pause and reflect on that for a moment before reading on. Perhaps even write some thoughts down.

I'm not going to suggest that, since Paul helped me develop the life blend model, life has been plain sailing and without its struggles.

It hasn't.

But it has provided a clear and simple picture of my life and helped me identify the different dimensions I need to be aware of, and how they interplay with each other.

It's removed my blinkers and helped me appreciate the larger story.

The reality is that life will rarely be balanced – but it can be well blended.

Great Life Tip

Become more intentional and less reactionary in how you're living your life.

So now the ball is in your court.

Recognize the importance of all aspects of your life; not only could it help you avoid burnout and break-ups, but success won't leave you with a bitter taste either.

We never did eat the prawn crackers or seaweed that Christmas Eve. But over 20 years on from that night, my wife Helen and I are still together.

That's the power of blend.

And a wise mentor.

Chapter 22

TWO PEOPLE YOU NEED IN LIFE

I learnt a new word recently: ultracrepidarianism. (Don't worry, I struggled to pronounce it too.) It means speaking with authority about subjects you know nothing about. If you're like me, you've probably met a few people like that. They appear on radio phone-ins, social media, and one or two of them even masquerade as politicians.

In my work I meet thousands of people every year, from a wide range of countries, cultures, and backgrounds. It's one of the main things I enjoy about my job. (Even those with ultracrepidarianism can sometimes be amusing.) Most are extremely brief encounters with people I'll never meet again, but one or two develop into long-term friendships. One guy, Matt, who I only met 18 months ago, has already become a very close friend whose wisdom and insights I value on a number of issues – including his thoughts on this book.

So, the words of the neuroscientist David Eagleman probably come as no surprise:

> There's no avoiding the truth etched into the wiring of our brains – we need each other.

That's so true, isn't it?

Great Life Insight

A great life is rarely, if ever, built alone.

It almost always requires the support of others, and the reality is our friends can play a significant part in shaping our lives whether we're aware of it or not.

The bottom line?

Your mates matter.

As indeed do the people you regularly spend time with, including your boss, your colleagues, and, of course, your family.

When you think about the people you regularly spend time with, hopefully most of them make a positive impact, but perhaps one or two of them less so.

For instance, there are people like 'the Awfuliser', the person who loves to dramatize issues and only seems happy when they're miserable. They can suck the life out of you as they seem intent on spreading their misery far and wide, often without fully appreciating the impact they're having on others. You have my sympathy if you work or live with such a person.

And there are certain people whose input into your life, even if not done consciously or intentionally, can have a profound influence and impact on you and your future.

I call them Cheerleaders and Challengers.

Cheerleaders are the people who believe in you and are always there to cheer you on in the good and the bad times. It's as if they carry around a self-belief tank which you can plug into whenever you need it. Friends can clearly be like this, but it can be especially powerful when a boss or someone you respect encourages you.

You see, sometimes it's not just what's said, but who says it that can be significant.

For example, I'm sure we're thrilled if our mum thinks we're a great singer and destined for success. But when Simon Cowell says it, it does carry a little more weight doesn't it?

Everyone loves having a Cheerleader. Having spoken in 41 countries in the last 26 years, I've yet to come across anyone who's said, 'My trouble is I've had too much encouragement in life.'

However, the temptation is that's the only voice we want to hear.

Norman Vincent Peale wrote:

> The trouble with most of us is that we would rather be ruined by praise than saved by criticism.

I think he may have a point.

That's why we also need Challengers in our lives.

What do they do? Something crucial.

Great Life Insight

Challengers tell you what you need to hear, not necessarily what you want to hear.

For example, one of the ways a Challenger can help you is by rescuing you from the dangers of confirmation bias, where you seek out information and ideas that already support your own. If left unchecked, confirmation bias can give you a distorted and unbalanced view of life. However,

Challengers can provide you with an alternative perspective, one that might not necessarily fit your current worldview. They can help you see things you might not normally see and can challenge, at times, both your attitudes and actions.

It's worth reflecting on who the Cheerleaders and Challengers in your life are. Do you have any? Some people can play either one role or the other, but some can play both. The problem occurs when we have neither.

When that happens, we're left having to be our own Cheerleader and Challenger – and that's not always easy.

For myself, I appreciate my Cheerleaders, but I know it's my Challengers who can add even greater value to my life.

Why?

Well, I'm fortunate that my self-belief tank is not running close to empty. I'm grateful that, because of the nature of my work, I do receive encouragement and appreciation from others on a regular basis.

But for my own growth I recognize Challengers bring a different perspective to my world and I value working with and talking to people who are willing to ask tough questions of me, challenge my assumptions, and offer an alternative perspective to my own.

I'll be honest. It's not always an easy exchange, but it's one I know I benefit from.

For instance, each member of my team will have read this manuscript before it was submitted to the publisher. Although I'd love them to tell me how great the book is, I'm conscious that the real value they provide is when they raise an issue I'd not considered and are prepared to challenge what I've written.

But here's something really important.

I'm also very aware of their heart and intention behind their feedback.

They're not intending to be awkward (I don't think so anyway) but are simply wanting this to be the best book it can possibly be.

So, if you're not enjoying it, don't forget to email Kev, Sally, Matt, Ed, Catriona, and Helen with your comments – because they're the ones to blame.

Having said that, there was a time when my self-belief tank wasn't so full. A pivotal moment in my career came when a woman called Jacqueline Guthrie, having seen me present my first ever public seminar on behalf of her company, stated 'Today was not a brilliant experience, but I saw enough potential in you to believe you can become one of our top presenters.'

Trust me, words have the power to bring life and hope as well as doubt and fear. Jacqueline's definitely brought the former.

She wasn't my Cheerleader purely for the sake of being so. She had a wealth of experience that I respected. She could have focused purely on challenging me. But after what had not been the easiest of days for me, her words gave me the confidence and self-belief to drive forward with my career.

You see, even those outwardly confident extroverts need Cheerleaders at some point in their lives.

However, if we ignore our Challengers or never seek out their opinion, then it becomes easy to fall into the trap of self-delusion – particularly if you're already in a role where you regularly receive praise from others. This can breed both complacency and arrogance.

And that won't help you develop or sustain a great life.

So, remember, your mates and the people you spend time with matter.

I hope you're fortunate to be able to count upon your Cheerleaders, but make sure you also have your Challengers, who want you to become the best version of you that you can be – and are prepared to challenge you in order to help you achieve it.

Chapter 23

PRUNE BACK THE HAPPY CLAPPY TREE SOMETIMES

I'm always curious as to why an organization hires me to speak at its conference. There are hundreds of celebrity speakers to choose from, especially from the world of sport. (My one and only sporting achievement was third place in the sack race at school when I was six. Shamefully, I was actually disqualified for cheating in the egg and spoon race that year, a decision I still contest to this day.)

Julie, one organizer who had hired me for her conference, explained their reasons as follows:

'We've had either mountaineers or sportspeople for the last few years. They've always had inspiring stories to tell, but if I'm honest the staff don't always relate to them.

I mean, overcoming frostbite is amazing, but it's not a challenge my sales team face very often.

We've chosen you because they'll appreciate your down-to-earthness and your humour. They do want a laugh and to feel inspired, but they also need practical, real-world examples they can relate to. So, it needs to be positive, but it's got to be realistic too, otherwise they just switch off.'

Interesting, eh?

You see, I think that can be the danger with positivity sometimes – it's not always grounded in reality. It's often caught up somewhere in the clouds, detached from the real world.

Now don't get me wrong, I'm a big believer in the importance of a positive attitude and I recognize there's too much cynicism around for our own good.

But I actually think there's still room for what I call 'appropriate pessimism' (to get more of an understanding of this, check out the chapter 'Not All Worries Are Worthless') and even a dose of scepticism on occasions.

Here's the deal:

Great Life Insight

Blind optimism needs eyes.

What does that mean in reality? It means it's great to dream big and have high aspirations, but if I'm honest, sometimes telling people you can be anything you want to be doesn't necessarily fuel desire – it helps give birth to delusions. And in some situations, it's understanding that caution can be just as important as courage.

I did once briefly join a happy clappy commune. I was part of a project team with Mike, Andy, and Nicola.

Boy were we positive.

The energy in the room during one of our team meetings could be likened to a troop of kangaroos on steroids. None of us could sit still.

We had so many ideas and were constantly jumping up to write down our thoughts on the flipchart.

Mike, our leader, was particularly pumped up. His favourite phrase was 'That's amazing' – which I confess lost its impact somewhat when he used it to describe the egg mayonnaise sandwiches we had at lunch.

Now having initially been caught up in this wave of gushing positivity, eventually shards of doubt began to penetrate the surface of my thinking.

Of course, I quickly had to suppress them because, as Nicola said, 'You can't afford the luxury of a negative thought.' And believe me, within this group one of the biggest crimes you could commit against humanity was to be negative.

So, what happened? The group disbanded a few weeks later. The project failed to get off the ground.

Mike moved on to 'an amazing' company without even a goodbye. Nicola remained but blamed the failure on a lack of support from senior management.

I was less convinced.

You see, we were a group of like-minded people, who read the same books, listened to the same motivational speakers, and all laughed at the people we labelled BMWs (Bitching, Moaning, Whingers).

And that was the problem. Our naïve positivity also created an air of arrogance and misplaced invincibility.

Our attitude was 'What on earth could go wrong?'

As a result, we didn't challenge each other.

There was no 'reality checker' within the group who could make sure we tested and analysed ideas before racing ahead to implement them. There was no one to say, 'Hang on a minute, what do we do if this happens?'

We didn't anticipate problems, we just refused to believe they existed.

How I wish we had pruned back on our positivity at times and allowed other perspectives to grow.

Now let me be clear, positivity can be powerful. It's absolutely crucial to our sense of wellbeing. Being caught up in a cycle of negativity is demoralizing.

So I'm not suggesting we board the negativity train, calling at despair, disillusionment, despondency, and discouragement – with a free moaning zone in every carriage.

That's not what I'm saying.

But this next point is crucial.

Great Life Insight

Remember, positivity is a key ingredient in creating a great life, but it's not the only one.

A cake can taste sickly if you add too much sugar, so you need other ingredients to balance the flavour.

And it's the same with life. Positivity will always be crucial, but prune it back sometimes and allow a little room for doubt, for being challenged, and yes, even for some appropriate pessimism on occasions, because together they can help us to deal with whatever challenges life may throw at us. And that's the recipe you need to have a great life.

Chapter 24

DON'T BE A TOAT

There's a guy I see at the gym called Jim. Yes, that's right, I see Jim at the gym. I'm there to sweat, stretch, and curb the after effects of too many carbs. Jim's there to talk to anyone and everyone. And his main topic of conversation? Himself.

I know a great deal about Jim, particularly his illnesses, but I doubt he knows anything about me. Why? He's never asked.

I wonder if you've ever spent time in conversation with someone like Jim and realized it's not actually a conversation you're having – it's just you listening to them delivering a monologue?

Let's be honest, there are lots of people who are comfortable being the centre of attention and dominating the conversation. And I'm sure you know someone like that, don't you?

And that's fine, if what they have to say is engaging and of interest to you. It's also acceptable if, having occupied centre-stage for a while, they then take a back seat and offer you some time in the spotlight.

But what about when that doesn't happen? What about when the monologue continues while you wait patiently in the wings?

It's not a great experience, is it? In fact, it can become rather boring and monotonous, and has the potential to make that person's likeability evaporate rapidly.

Well, I have a name for such people. They're what I affectionately call a TOAT – Talk Only About Themselves.

Hey, talking about ourselves can be an enjoyable thing to do. I've probably been a TOAT myself on occasions. Maybe we all have. And possibly for good reasons. We may have friends who love finding out our news but for whatever reason feel reticent to share theirs, hence we do most of the talking. Or perhaps at times we've been struggling, needed to vent, and had a friend who was just happy to listen. That's fine, it happens.

But then there are examples of people who are constant TOATs. They're the ones who, when they do finally give you the space to talk, pounce on the slightest opportunity to hijack what you're saying and bring the conversation back to themselves.

Ever come across those people? TOATs that hijack?

I guess the challenge is this. How often are you a TOAT? How often are you giving people in your world time to talk about themselves?

Here's the deal: what ultimately brings us fulfilment and happiness in life is our relationships with others.

Great Life Insight

One of the clearest ways you can show you value and respect another person is to show genuine interest in them.

You see, it really is important to remind yourself that it's not all about you.

It's about us.

My wife Helen is a brilliant listener. She's genuinely interested in others, and perhaps you are too. However, take a moment to reflect on some of your recent conversations, both in a personal and a work context.

How much genuine listening did you do? Were you listening or just waiting for your turn to talk? How much do you really know about what's going on in the other person's world? How often did you bring the conversation back to yourself?

Believe me, I know I'm prone to being more than an occasional TOAT. But equally, I've developed the awareness to realize that about myself. That's why now when meeting for a catch-up with friends I'm likely to begin by saying 'let's start with your news' – I want to give them the opportunity to be in the spotlight. And when I do get into the flow of conversation and realize I've been taking up most of the airtime, I might interject by saying 'Look, I've talked enough, what else has been happening with you?'

So when do you know people have had enough of you talking?

When they stop asking questions. If they're still asking questions then they're usually listening out of interest, not under duress.

Another, less subtle sign to be aware of though is when they start checking their phone but say 'go on, I'm listening'.

Poking their eyeballs with a pen whilst rocking in their chair is another sign.

So let's be clear. Talk about yourself by all means. Let your voice be heard, but make sure it's not the only voice that's heard. And when you are talking, make sure the topic is not always centred on you. Find out about other people's worlds – it will strengthen your connection, people will warm to you more as a result, and you may learn something really interesting about someone else.

Great Life Challenge

Are there some relationships in your world that could be enhanced by you doing a little less talking and a little more listening?

If you want a great life, don't be a TOAT. It's not all about you.

It's about other people too.

Are you listening Jim?

Chapter 25

NOT EVERYONE DRINKS WHISKY

It's great to be shown appreciation, isn't it? It can feel hugely satisfying to have your efforts recognized in some way, and to feel valued by others. But have you ever received a gift and wondered 'what am I supposed to do with this?' You might appreciate the sentiment. But the gift itself? Perhaps less so. That might explain the look on my face when, on a trip back from the Middle East, the conference organizer presented me with a large bouquet of flowers just as I was about to board my plane home.

Last Christmas I received a large bottle of whisky from a client. They wanted to say thank you for the work I had done with them earlier in the year. It included a handwritten letter explaining that it was an exceptional whisky that they hoped I would enjoy as much as they did. It was a kind and generous gift.

Of course, there was just one problem wasn't there?

I don't drink whisky.

Now contrast this with Richard, a speaker friend of mine, who contacted my office a month before Christmas and spoke to one of my team. He wanted to send me a gift as a thank you for some work I had referred to him. He asked my colleague Kev what my favourite drink was. Apparently, Richard was partial to a red wine and he had a sneaky feeling that I would share similar tastes. However, Kev tipped him off that I was actually a fan of Belgian beer and pale ale.

A month later I received a box of my favourite ales.

OK, so what's my taste in alcohol got to do with you having a great life?

It's simply this:

While it's great as a general starting point to 'treat people as you want to be treated', it's actually even more helpful to treat people as *they* want to be treated. And that's crucial to remember because...

Great Life Insight

The quality of our relationships is the key to us enjoying a great life.

So, for instance, if I have received some bad news I want to be on my own. I need time and space to process it. My wife, on the other hand, wants to talk things through. If I treat her the way *I* want to be treated: i.e. walk away and give her time alone, she'll consider that both rude and unhelpful. So, I need to support her in the way she appreciates, even if that's not the way I would want to be supported.

The reality is, what floats your boat might not float other people's. What motivates you might actually demotivate others. And whilst you may enjoy being the centre of attention, other people may positively hate it.

So, if you want to build better relationships with others the key is to...

Great Life Tip

Find out what's important to people. Discover what they value and do your best to satisfy those needs.

Here's an interesting perspective on how this might work in our close relationships with others. In his bestselling book *The 5 Love Languages* the author and counsellor Gary Chapman highlights five ways in which people like to express and experience love. They are as follows:

- Words of affirmation (either spoken or written down).

- Acts of service (actions speak louder than words).

- Receiving gifts (with the thought behind them being particularly important).

- Quality time (giving people your undivided attention).

- Physical touch (of course it has to be appropriate – a bear hug doesn't do it for everyone).

Chapman argues that our natural way to express our love to others is to do so in the way we like to have love expressed to us.

In other words, treat people as we would want to be treated.

So, if we like to receive gifts, we will normally want to give gifts to those we love. However, the challenge is that although gifts might be appreciated, the other person might actually place more value on 'acts of service' – being cooked their favourite meal, for example.

Chapman's point is to communicate love in the preferred language of the one receiving it – in other words, treat people as *they* want to be treated.

Chapman's book has sold over 11 million copies and although there's been a lack of academic research to test the validity of his model, thousands of couples have testified to the benefit of his work and how it's helped their relationships.

My own take is that Chapman's work does provide some food for thought and above all has the potential to open up the channels of communication between people. But I don't think it's helpful to try and make it into an exact science.

You see, I'm aware that people may have a number of different love languages and context may be a determining factor rather than simply personal preference.

For example, when I'm tired and my wife offers to make dinner (or even just a cup of tea) I value that more than on other occasions when I'm less tired. When I've been working away from home, my wife appreciates quality time more than when I've been office based for two weeks (in which case she's encouraging me to work away so she can catch up on her episodes of *Casualty*).

OK, so what happens if you're not sure how people want to be treated?

Do the obvious.

Ask them.

Here's a great question that takes the guesswork out of communication:

Great Life Tip

> Ask people 'If there's one thing I could do to help you now, what would it be?'

Ultimately, the heart of your happiness is based on your ability to build deep and meaningful relationships. So, let's become more conscious of treating people in a way that they value and is most meaningful and helpful to them at the time.

That may well tie in with your needs too, but not always. So please don't assume that what makes you happy is exactly the same as what makes others happy. It isn't always.

Remember, not everyone drinks whisky.

Chapter 26

DON'T WAIT FOR SOMEBODY'S FUNERAL

It was a bizarre experience as I lay on the operating table and the surgeon walked into the theatre and greeted me. His attempt at small talk and putting me at ease was as follows:

'I understand you're a motivational speaker.'

'Yes, that's one label people like to give me', I replied.

'Well I could certainly do with a bit of motivation', he said, without a hint of a smile.

I suddenly felt an overwhelming desire to get up and run, and my anxiety levels, which were already high, increased tenfold.

I wondered what he would have said if I worked as a funeral director. Perhaps some joke about coffins? The mind boggles.

I do wonder how much of a conversation stopper it must be when you say you work in the funeral industry. Death is not a topic many of us like to talk about generally. However, as I approach my mid-fifties, going to funerals has become more commonplace for me than weddings.

I've been to several in the last few years. Some have left me feeling completely devastated, and I've even helped carry the coffin on a few occasions.

Now although funerals can differ greatly from each other, there's usually a point during the ceremony when someone will say something about the deceased.

When my friend and colleague Vicky died, nine people spoke at her funeral, including her children. It was an incredibly emotional and moving time, which also included moments of laughter.

Other eulogies I've heard have been extremely brief, and on occasions even delivered by someone who didn't know the person they were talking about.

But there's something they all have in common.

They are not used as opportunities to criticize or settle scores with the deceased (well, not in my experience anyway) but rather as a time to recall some more positive memories about them.

I've yet to hear anyone say, 'To be honest, I couldn't stand the bloke' or 'I'd like to think of something positive to say about her, but my parents told me never to lie.'

Hey, even if we didn't particularly like the person we're talking about, we usually hold back on the criticism and emphasize the positives.

Or is that just me?

But here's an interesting point made by the author Eric Barker:

Great Life Insight

'Eulogies are so much more valuable when we do them before someone goes.'

I think he's got a point. Why wait for somebody's funeral before we say how much we appreciate them, or what we value about them as a person?

In recent years, as I become older and the reality of people's mortality becomes more apparent, I've begun to consciously let people know that I value them.

Now don't get me wrong. I don't call round to their house unannounced in a hearse armed with a large wreath and read out a 14-page eulogy (that didn't go down well the first time), but I am more likely to send them an encouraging text, write them a card, or mention something in conversation.

Yes, I'm mindful that some people can find this a little embarrassing, or even unusual – which is why a card, email, or text might be easier than saying something face to face. But no one has ever appeared upset or ungrateful.

I will always treasure the card my late friend Vicky sent me for my 50th birthday in which she expressed her gratitude for our friendship and was incredibly encouraging about the work I was doing.

Sadly, she wasn't around for my 51st.

But I know how I feel when I re-read her words, and I don't think I'm unusual in doing so.

I've even started to encourage and thank people I hardly know.

When my son was 15 he decided he wanted to become a doctor. The strange thing was that up until that point he hadn't liked biology (which I thought could be a pretty useful subject if you wanted to become a doctor).

But then something happened.

He got a new teacher, Mrs Shaw.

Her passion for the subject inspired him, and several years later my son is now a doctor.

I actually speak about Mrs Shaw in some of my talks. I use her as an example of the fact that one person can be MAD – Making A Difference. But it occurred to me that, despite singing Mrs Shaw's praises for several years, I had never met her or thanked her personally for the impact she'd made on my son.

So, I sent her a card.

I wrote a few words expressing my gratitude and how she had been the catalyst for my son wanting to become a doctor. I told her she was MAD, and I explained what the acronym meant. In all honesty I didn't expect to hear back from Mrs Shaw.

But I did.

She mentioned how grateful she was to hear from me and to discover what Matt was now doing. Her final words made a deep impression on me:

'Your card just made my year.'

Wow. We had never even met. We still haven't.

But I'm glad she heard those words of encouragement whilst she's still teaching. Who knows the impact they had, and perhaps still have, on her.

You see, Mrs Shaw is like all of us.

Great Life Insight

We all need the oxygen of encouragement occasionally.

So, remember, people are not always aware what's going on inside your head. They might not fully appreciate how much you value them.

But you can change that.

How you do that is up to you, just make sure you do it with sincerity and not with an expectation that you'll receive anything in return. That's not the point of the exercise.

Trust me, not only will you make a difference to them but to yourself also. The reality is, we feel good when we make others feel good. And that's yet another essential ingredient in helping us live a great life.

So, don't wait for somebody's funeral.

Great Life Challenge

Choose two people who you want to express your gratitude to. Think of a way in which you can do that. Be as simple or as extravagant as you wish – but don't just think about it. Do it.

Chapter 27

PLEASE RESIGN FROM THIS JOB

I've been driving for well over 30 years. I would hate to contemplate how many miles I've covered in that time, but I'm sure I could have comfortably driven to the moon and back. And whilst I enjoy driving most of the time, I have to confess it can be an entirely different experience when I'm a passenger.

On a recent trip abroad, it did cross my mind that I might be making an earlier departure from this planet than I'd intended. I was travelling in a taxi where it seemed the driver either had a death wish or a desperate need for the toilet. On several occasions I found my leg thrusting down hard on the non-existent brake pedal beneath me.

It's fair to say my stress levels soared.

Continuing on the driving theme, I'm no expert on the sport, but I understand one of the most stressful parts of a Formula 1 race for the driver is during the pit stop.

Why?

They're not in control. They're relying on someone else.

Admittedly they're relying on a highly trained team, but even so, the abdication of control, even for just a few seconds, can see an increase in their stress levels. Certainly my lack of control in that taxi was the cause of my sweaty palms and soaring heart rate.

The bottom line?

We like to be in control.

And there's nothing wrong with that need.

However, the challenge is when we want constantly to control people and situations in a way that meets our agenda and we're only happy when things are going exactly as we want them to. Taken to extremes, the result can be that we become increasingly controlling of others with a tendency to micromanage and interfere. And that can happen not only in work but also in our personal lives.

Believe me, that's not an ideal recipe for building better relationships or getting the best from others. And I wouldn't recommend it for your own stress levels either. Here's the deal:

Great Life Insight

If you want to live a great life you need to resign from being general manager of the universe.

Now that doesn't mean a complete abdication of your responsibilities. For instance, if you're a parent with young children it's fairly obvious you'll need to be hands on and exert high levels of influence and control, often for their own safety. However, as children get older we need to make sure how we parent them adapts. Being too highly controlling can potentially sow the seeds of rebellion in young people, and create an environment where conflict is commonplace.

This need to be less controlling and more flexible and adaptable relates to all aspects of our lives.

When I started my own business I did everything. I ordered supplies, kept my accounts, sent out invoices, did all my own marketing, and developed and delivered all my own training. And in a world where PowerPoint didn't exist, I even designed my own acetates for the overhead projector. (Never used an overhead projector? You haven't lived.)

As the business grew, my wife became increasingly involved, and then further people were added to the team. Yet, for some time I would still read every email and allow myself to become drawn into situations that were being handled by someone else. It's tempting to do, believe me.

Becoming less involved was difficult. Allowing other people to get on with their jobs so I was free to get on with my own did not come easily. The result was a combination of long hours and increased stress.

However, a bit like that pit stop crew from the Formula 1 race, I realized over time that my team's training and experience meant they could be relied upon and needed less input from me. As a result, both my stress levels and working hours decreased. And it probably did a lot for their job satisfaction too, knowing that I had confidence in them.

But that doesn't mean I've abdicated complete control.

We still have regular team meetings. There are times when I still need to be involved in the detail of certain projects, but I've learnt to relax more. To trust more. Here's my biggest lesson learnt:

I need to control some things, but I don't need to be in control of everything. The skill, of course, is to know where to focus my influence. And that only comes when I know my strengths and those of my team.

So, what about you? Take a moment to reflect on both your work life and your personal life.

Where do you need to ease back on the controls? What are the consequences if you don't? Who else, apart from you, benefits if you do?

Here's the deal: the world was here before you; for several billion years in fact.

So ...

Great Life Insight

Remember, people on this planet managed to get on with life before you arrived, and the reality is they will continue to do so after you've gone.

Obsessive controlling can be both exhausting and draining for you. And it can be frustrating and demoralizing for others. So maybe lighten up a bit in some areas. Be prepared to let go of certain things and situations. Continue to be committed to life, but give people more freedom and responsibility, particularly in your personal life. Allow them to develop; to grow. They have their own lives to lead and their decisions to make. They won't always please you. Some of what they do might even pain you. They'll make mistakes. So, by all means offer support, suggest ideas, and share your wisdom – just recognize that your job is not to be the general manager of their universe. And if it is, for their sake and yours, you need to hand in your resignation. Immediately.

Chapter 28

A CRUCIAL FORMULA YOU NEED TO KNOW

As you may have gathered by now, my car is my second home. I get to eat, drink, and on occasion even sleep in it (although I hasten to add I only do the latter when I'm stationary). At times it feels like I'm mates with most motorway service station staff throughout the UK, and it's tempting to see all these hours travelling as the downside to my job. But, actually, it's quite the opposite.

I use it as a chance to catch up with friends on the phone, enjoy my daily consumption of sports news via the radio, and also to learn. In my early days of business my car became 'a university on wheels' as I listened to endless hours of business and life wisdom, invariably from men and women from across the pond. Some of their ideas were a little wacky (I never did do the naked mirror exercise – that's a story for another book). But overall, the insight and motivation they provided was crucial to me as I worked hard to get my business established.

One set of talks I remember listening to was by the author and speaker Jack Canfield. He became famous for co-authoring the 'Chicken Soup for the Soul' series. In his audio programme *Self Esteem and Peak Performance* he shared a particular formula that is embarrassingly simple but also incredibly powerful. The formula was E+R=O.

Great Life Insight

It's the Event plus my Response that determines the Outcome.

I guess that's pretty obvious in hindsight, but of all the ideas I've acquired over the years this has had a deep, long-lasting impact on me.

In a nutshell, events happen in our lives. Some are pretty good, some are fairly indifferent, and others can be particularly challenging. However, it's not solely the Event that determines the Outcome, but how we Respond to it.

So, for instance, perhaps someone forgets our birthday, fails to return a call, or seems a little offhand when you meet up for a drink. These are the events. But what happens next is not based solely on what's happened – it's based on how we respond.

So, we could make light of the issue and quickly dismiss it, recognizing there could be a whole host of reasons for why the other person behaved the way they did. Alternatively, we could take offence and allow ourselves to be hurt and when we do have contact with them, be a little cool. This response could escalate the issue and potentially have a negative impact on the relationship.

Interesting, isn't it? Same events. Different outcomes.

Why? Because of how we responded.

I wonder, in which particular situations in your life do you think this formula would be worth remembering?

For me, I realize I've been quick to blame other people for how I'm feeling. When my children were younger it's fair to say I wasn't always the calmest and most laid back of parents. I worked from home, in a house where kids' toys seemed to end up everywhere but in the toy box, and where my then three-year-old daughter would have a tantrum if I didn't let her answer the business phone. It felt like a rich breeding ground for high stress levels, and it wasn't helped by the fact that my response was often to play the role of victim and place all the blame for my stress on my wife and children.

However, when I eventually quit being the victim of the situation, it occurred to me that one of two things needed to happen. I could influence the 'event' and work away from home in rented office space, or alternatively ask the kids to move out (which did seem a little harsh as they were both under six). Or I could work on my response to the event. That would involve deciding not to place all the blame on my family for my stress, starting to manage my day better, and having a different phone line installed.

That was it in a nutshell – either do something about the event or do something about my response.

So, what did I do?

I chose to work on my response (partly because we couldn't afford a new place for the children and my wife said she'd miss them).

Now I didn't suddenly transform into some calm mystic guru who floated effortlessly around the house. And if I'm honest, I did find it hard initially. But I realized the following:

Great Life Tip

Take more responsibility for how you respond to situations rather than continually playing the blame game.

This formula stood me in good stead a few years later when my business received what I considered to be unjustified negative publicity. My first reaction was to send out invites to the pity party and order a stack of victim T-shirts. But that would not have improved the situation even if I felt justified in doing so. What I did instead was take ownership for how we responded as a team. It was not a time to play the victim, but to respond as a leader. With the support of my team not only did we manage the situation really well, but our business actually grew as a result.

It's very easy to blame people and situations (the Event) for where we find ourselves in life (our Outcomes). But remember, the formula isn't $E = O$ (Event = Outcome). It's $E + R = O$. We are part of the formula.

Great Life Insight

Our responses matter.

The reality is, we can't always change the event, but we can work on how we respond to it.

That doesn't mean we don't hold people accountable for their behaviour or passively accept a situation. It does mean we recognize that outcomes aren't inevitable; it's through our response that we get to shape them.

You might want to check out some of the responses you've been making to situations going on in your life right now. Is it possible you're playing the blame game? Are you passively accepting a situation rather than thinking how a change of response by you might improve the outcome? Maybe you're leaving it to fate or other people to determine your future. Maybe you're hoping 'events' will just magically improve or disappear. Either way, if you want to have a great life, take ownership of your responses.

E + R = O. It may be a very simple formula, but believe me, it's incredibly empowering.

Chapter 29

A FOOL-PROOF WAY TO AVOID CRITICISM

Let me ask you a question. Imagine if every piece of written work you had ever done at school or at work was made public to the world and people were free to pass comment on it. So that's every piece of homework, every essay, exam paper, report, client proposal etc. Not only that, but imagine if the comments people made about your work, whether positive or negative, encouraging or nasty, could be read by anyone else.

Let that thought sink in for a moment.

Seriously, how would you feel?

It would be a weird feeling, to have your work scrutinized so publicly, wouldn't it? But for an author it's not weird – it's reality.

I first started writing books in the early 1990s. It was a world before Facebook, Twitter, iPhones and, the interesting one for me as an author, Amazon.

Writing a book prior to Amazon's arrival in July 1994 meant you hoped it would find its way into a bookshop, and that those reading it would have nice things to say about it and would spread the word.

But the arrival of Amazon changed the game completely. Books were now easier to purchase, and, as people increasingly embraced the internet, it provided a stage for them to voice their opinion to a global audience. Now not only could my books be bought online, but they could also be reviewed by anyone (even if they hadn't read the book) and these reviews were available for the world to see. So, writing a book in the internet age helps you reach a wider audience than ever before – and it also creates the opportunity for people to publicly praise or criticize your work like never before.

I'll be honest, it's thrilling to see your book on Amazon and hopefully see it move up the charts. I've even been fortunate to see a few of my books appear in the bestsellers list. (My mum buys a lot of copies.) I didn't hesitate to take a screen shot when that happened.

But there's another side to the story.

You see, beyond the pride and satisfaction of seeing your book published, for me and, I think, for other authors, there can also be an underlying dread.

What if people don't like your book?

Prior to July 1994, their comments would have remained largely with the people they knew personally. But not anymore.

Now the whole world can know, and having received several hundred reviews of my books, I'm aware that people don't pull any punches with their comments. Their criticisms can be both biting and personal. Now I'm glad to say the vast majority are extremely positive – but guess which ones I tend to focus on and remember?

I guess that's the price you pay when you put yourself and your work 'out there'. You create an opportunity for people to praise or criticize your work. And criticism is not easy to receive – especially when it's done publicly. But relax, because there is a way to avoid it. It's simply this:

Do nothing. Be nothing. Say nothing.

Remain anonymous. Remain in the shadows.

It's hard to be criticized when no one knows you're there. It's difficult to disagree with you and challenge you when you have nothing to say,

It's almost a fool-proof way to avoid criticism. But it's hardly a recipe for success, is it?

I'm guessing your goal is not to pussyfoot your way through the vast array of life's opportunities with the sole purpose of never upsetting anyone, is it?

Now I'm not suggesting we should go out of our way to deliberately upset and annoy people (although it does come naturally to some). I also recognize that criticism, whilst not always welcome, can actually be helpful. But …

Great Life Insight

If you want to achieve anything in life, there's a good chance you'll acquire some critics along the way.

I love the response Elizabeth Gilbert gave to a critic of her book *Eat Pray Love*:

> I hate to get metaphysical about this but we are here for such a short time. We are mortal and it's over before you know it. I just can't give a shit where people put me in the filing cabinet of their own imagination … The clock is ticking, we have to limit where we put our energies and resources, and I'm not going to put them into caring what other people think of me.

Will we ever get used to criticism? Some people possibly will – particularly politicians. For others, it may always be a challenge. But when it does happen, and when others do knock you, remember that these bumps and bruises are a sign that you're participating in life. You're still in the game, not hiding on the sidelines.

And remember the alternative:

Do nothing. Be nothing. Say nothing.

It's not exactly a strategy for success, fulfilment, or happiness. But it is a fool-proof way to avoid criticism.

Chapter 30

YOU WON'T BE MATES WITH EVERYONE

Bridgette arrived early for my workshop, while I was still setting up the room.

It was the first time we had met.

We exchanged some brief pleasantries whilst she grabbed a coffee, sat down, and opened her newspaper.

Five minutes later I was all prepared, so I wandered over to Bridgette armed with my friendly smile and a small plate of ginger biscuits. As I did so, I noticed her paper was open at the property section. Wanting to initiate some small talk and seeing her lack of interest in the ginger biscuits, I asked:

'Oh, so thinking of moving house are you?'

Bridgette's reply was both swift and unforgettable.

'Is that any of your bloody business?'

Now call me intuitive, but I sensed Bridgette wasn't up for small talk. (I've always been quick on the uptake.)

It was a relief when her colleagues arrived shortly after and the awkward silence that filled the room was soon replaced by laughter and conversation. It proved to be a really good day.

Bridgette's colleagues were engaged and eager to learn, which was reflected in their feedback. However, I wasn't entirely surprised when I read Bridgette's evaluation form. I think it's fair to say she wasn't my biggest fan, and she was highly critical of the whole day.

It was a long drive home after that workshop, and all I could think of was my encounter with Bridgette as I constantly replayed her comments over and over in my head.

That was a few years ago, and in that time I've met one or two more people like Bridgette. It's never a great experience when you receive criticism, especially when you think it's unjustified. But experience has taught me a few things.

Firstly, it's taught me to weigh up the criticism I receive rather than instantly dismiss it.

Secondly, I've learnt that not everyone will like me or my style. So, I need to give up on my constant quest to please everyone.

For a start, I'll never succeed. But I will endure sleepless nights and plenty of stress in my efforts to do so.

Not everyone appreciates my phrase SUMO (Shut Up, Move On), despite my attempts to assure them it's not as aggressive as it may sound. But my speaker friend Kirsty Spraggon had some great advice for me. She wrote:

> Don't cater to those who won't get your message or who will be offended – they don't resonate with it for a reason. Just trust that the ones who are supposed to get it will.

Her words lifted a burden off my shoulders. In life I won't be mates with everyone. And neither will you. But guess what? That's OK.

Great Life Insight

Some people won't like you. Period. They might even be struggling to like themselves.

Of course, it's not easy to be rejected. Being socially excluded activates the same part of the brain that's activated when we are physically hurt. So, no wonder we get defensive about criticism at times. And it's upsetting when, despite all your best efforts, some people choose to dislike you.

Our brains have evolved to notice the negatives. Hence, one negative comment impacts us more than 10 positive ones. That's why it's so important (although not always easy) to get things in perspective and remind yourself of the positive relationships you do have. (Although to be fair, if it seems everyone dislikes you, then you probably do have a serious problem.)

So, for me, my relationships with my wife, children, and close friends are crucial. I'm going to pay more attention to their opinion of me compared to that of a stranger who I'm unlikely ever to meet again.

And remember, political parties are often swept to power despite receiving less than 50% of the vote. That's a high percentage of people who didn't vote for them, but they still achieved power.

And the lesson from that is ...?

Being successful doesn't mean you'll receive everyone's approval.

So, take my advice:

Great Life Tip

Stop wasting your time
and emotional energy always
trying to please everyone.
You're here to make
a difference, not to win
a popularity contest.

And also, be careful you don't waste your energy resenting the people who dislike you.

Remember, you're travelling your journey and they're travelling theirs.

I respect Bridgette's right to her opinion, but I chose not to act on it. Her comments on the evaluation form advised me to quit what I was doing and join the real world. Our paths never crossed again, but I can understand why her manager felt she would benefit from my workshop.

Did I mention the title of it?

'Building Winning Relationships with Customers and Colleagues'

Here's the deal:

If you spend your life trying to make everyone else happy, you'll never be happy. And that's not a recipe for a great life, is it?

So, do yourself a favour and get used to the fact.

You won't be mates with everyone.

Chapter 31

MANAGE YOUR MENTAL DIET

My daughter Ruth used to play the piano when she was younger. But she's now 22 and those keys have remained untouched for several years. Until recently.

Her first attempt at playing a tune could understandably best be described as rusty. She became a little discouraged.

Then something interesting happened.

For my birthday Ruth decided to buy me an old-fashioned coffee tin and place in it 52 motivational and inspirational quotes. So, every Monday morning, rather than me simply relying on a cup of coffee for a boost (or a Premier Inn cooked breakfast), I could pick a quote to set me up for the week.

Now Ruth spent a few days searching for these quotes, choosing 52 of them and then writing them down. Perhaps without even realizing it, she was feeding her own mind with some really helpful thoughts.

And guess what?

She went back to her piano and managed to play a tune she'd often struggled to play as a child.

Great Life Insight

There's something really powerful and profound about the thoughts we have.

The reality is that the internal conversations we have with ourselves matter more than we ever realize.

So, here are a couple of questions for you to ponder:

> How's your mental diet? Is it nourishing and fuelling your motivation, mood, and morale?

> Are your internal conversations helping or harming
> your pursuit of a great life?

In terms of our physical health we're encouraged to check what we eat and limit the amount of certain foods we consume. That's great advice for our physical wellbeing, but let's explore two ways we can help improve our own mental diet and, as a result, improve our mental and emotional wellbeing.

Gear Yourself up with Gratitude

Google the phrase 'the science of gratitude' and you'll be inundated with academic studies hailing the benefits of gratitude. Research, in particular by Robert Emmons and Mike McCullogh, from the University of California and Miami respectively, highlights the huge benefits of practising gratitude on a regular basis and its impact on our happiness, the quality of our relationships, and also our own levels of generosity.

So, if you're sceptical about its impact, just take a look at the scientific research.

Great Life Insight

Even the most hardened cynic would struggle to counter the overwhelming evidence of the benefits of practising gratitude.

So how can you weave this into your own life? I can only speak from personal experience, but here's what I do.

Firstly, before I get out of bed in the morning I reflect on my 'Thankful four' – that's four things from the previous day that I'm thankful for. And here's what's interesting:

I always struggle.

To only come up with four.

The reality is 'seek and you shall find', and when you start looking for things to be grateful for, your brain is more than happy to find them for you.

By doing this at the start of the day, I'm feeding my mind with a positive boost rather than abdicating that responsibility to whatever is on the news (which is rarely positive), or what mood I happen to wake up in. I'm taking responsibility for how I start my day.

Here's something else I've been doing for the last few years. I've developed a ritual whereby every Sunday morning I get my journal out (rather imaginatively called my Gratitude Journal) and recall anything from the week that caused me to smile. That can include absolutely anything, from catching up with a friend, enjoying a cuddle with my cats, a train that arrived on time, or the fact I saw some sunshine that week (not a regular occurrence in the North of England).

I've recorded loads in my journal, and it's incredibly satisfying to look back and read all that I've experienced and encountered in life – things that would have been so easy to forget if I hadn't taken the time to remember and record them.

How you decide to practise gratitude is up to you – just make sure you do it. Personally, I think such a practice should be part of the school curriculum, because whatever your age, everyone needs support in developing a healthy mental diet.

Have Kinder Conversations . . . with Yourself

I've worked with enough people to realize the following: some of our internal conversations aren't kind. In fact, they're cruel. It's easy to beat ourselves up because we're not always perfect, and to be our own worst critic rather than a helpful coach. Boy have I got the T-shirt for that. What about you?

The following phrases are the equivalent of feeding ourselves a diet of junk food:

> 'I'll never be good at ...'

> 'I'm such an idiot.'

> 'The teachers were right at school, I'll never make anything of my life.'

> 'I'm such a failure, I never learn.'

But there's some good news.

Just as you can change your physical diet, you can also change your mental one. You can choose a new diet immediately, and although it does take time to see the benefits, they will come. Trust me, I'm talking from experience.

So, start by injecting your internal conversations with more empowering, constructive, and compassionate language. How?

By taking the following supplements you'll give your mental diet a boost and in doing so, improve your own emotional wellbeing. Which of the following could you start taking regularly?

> 'I recognize I have some failings and I'm still an OK person.'

> 'I recognize and value the many qualities I have.'

> 'I'm making progress from where I was before.'

> 'I make mistakes, but mistakes don't make me.'

> 'I'm learning to become my own best friend.'

> 'I have the ability to improve from where I am now.'

Of course, you could develop your own phrases to start including in your diet. The key is to make sure you use them regularly. And if you do come up with your own phrases, why don't you email them to me – Paul.McGee@ theSUMOguy.com – I'd love to hear from you.

Great Life Insight

In order to have a great life we need to develop not only our skillset, but also our mindset.

How healthy your mindset is depends on what you've been feeding it.

So please don't become bloated on negativity but energize and nourish yourself with food that feeds the mind. To do so, gear yourself up with gratitude and please have kinder conversations … with yourself.

I'm sure my daughter's fingers were freed up when she started to play the piano, but I've a sneaky feeling her mindset was freed up too. And hearing her play was like food for my soul.

Chapter 32

BEWARE THE CURSE OF COMFORT

L et's start with a simple experiment. Now if you're reading this book in a crowded place, perhaps on a train or in a cafe, you might just want to do the following exercise in a subtle, understated way.

Ready?

Here goes.

Simply stretch out both hands in front of you, with your fingers pointing forwards. Now, clasp your hands together so that one thumb is on top of the other.

Now take a look at which thumb is on top: your right or your left?

If it's your right thumb then you're like me.

And you may have read recently that research suggests people who have their right thumb on top are usually more intelligent than their left thumb counterparts.

Honest.

OK, now separate out your hands again. However, this time, when you bring them back together, put whichever thumb was on the bottom last time (in my case, my left thumb) on top this time.

So how does that feel?

Most people say it feels strange. And even if they don't, they recognize doing it the second time round takes them slightly longer.

Now if you just did this exercise in a public place, you might want to take a moment to look around to see if anyone is looking at you in a suspicious way. If so, just smile politely and continue reading.

OK, so what's the point of this exercise?

Well, sometimes life can be similar to what we've just done. In other words, trying something different from our usual routine can feel strange.

And when this happens, the natural temptation is to revert to how you've always done it because that feels more comfortable.

Agree?

Of course, there's certainly no harm in sticking to what you're comfortable with, particularly when doing it differently has no real tangible benefit (your life is not about to change dramatically because you've swapped which thumb is now on top).

But could our desire for the familiar and the appeal of the status quo possibly be preventing us from having a great life? I think it could.

Psychologists tell us we all like our comfort zones, but here's the really interesting bit:

Great Life Insight

Research indicates that we don't always do what makes us happy, we tend to do what's easiest and most comfortable.

So, why's that the case?

Well, as you'll have discovered in other chapters, our brain is always looking for ways to save energy and also keep us safe. So, although a night out with friends could be what makes you happy, if it's a cold, wet night, the lure of television and a takeaway pizza might be the option you take instead.

Why?

It's the easiest and most comfortable option.

In her book, *Emotional Agility*, Susan David calls this the curse of comfort.

Of course, if you simply want the easy life, and that makes you feel happy and fulfilled, then who am I to argue? It's just I strongly suspect that if you decided to read this book then there's something within you that wants to do more than carry on doing whatever is easiest.

Am I right?

You see, when it comes to living a great life, a hugely important question to ask yourself is this:

'Where do life's opportunities really lie: inside or outside my comfort zone?'

If we're honest, I believe deep down we already know the answer to that question, don't we?

There's nothing wrong with operating in your comfort zone. Doing something regularly that you're familiar with can be both comforting and reassuring. But here's my question to you:

Are there times when you know you would like to try something new, or go somewhere different, but the comfort of routine prevents you from doing so?

Great Life Challenge

Has your comfort blanket actually become a straightjacket?

I think our tendency to do what's easiest rather than what makes us happy is more commonplace than we realize.

Let me elaborate.

I took my mum out for dinner recently to celebrate her 76th birthday. At the time, she was waiting for a knee replacement operation, and found walking difficult. She found getting up from a chair even harder.

On the way to our table my mum had spotted the desserts invitingly displayed in a glass cabinet. She took a moment to soak in the selection.

After our main course I asked if she wanted to go to the dessert display and choose something. To do so would mean getting off her chair, which she would find painful (although she would have to do it to leave the restaurant).

I knew she wanted a dessert, and although the chocolate cake looked tempting, I think the lemon meringue pie had her name on it.

I offered to assist her getting up and to walk her to the dessert display.

Her reply was 'It's OK Paul, it's too much trouble, I'll just have a coffee.'

Now there was no denying choosing a dessert would cause her some additional temporary pain, but it was her birthday and the dessert selection was huge. I wanted her to enjoy the occasion.

Don't get me wrong. I wasn't bullying her into getting a dessert, but I knew she would enjoy one. I gently encouraged her to do what I knew would make her happy.

And guess what?

She pushed through the pain barrier and loved her dessert. I've never seen a large piece of lemon meringue pie disappear so quickly.

So, I wonder, what's the equivalent of my mum's dessert for you?

You know you want something but you're also aware you might feel a degree of discomfort in getting it.

Maybe it means extra work on your part; maybe extra study. Perhaps it means meeting new people or going to places you've not been to previously.

I'm not suggesting you don't like what you're currently doing. But ...

Great Life Challenge

Is life offering us a much wider and larger menu than we're currently enjoying?

Have the main course and coffee by all means – but is there a dessert with your name on it that you know you would enjoy?

OK, I recognize the status quo can seem appealing, and it's understandable that at times we want to stick to the familiar path.

But just be aware of this:

We often feel at our best when the activities we're engaged in require us to stretch our abilities.

Great Life Insight

Fulfilment comes from successfully meeting challenges – not from always avoiding them.

I love this quote from the author and speaker Brene Brown.

Take time to ponder it.

> The big question I ask is, when I had the opportunity did I choose courage over comfort?

Here's the deal:

Life is an incredible privilege that comes with many challenges, as well as amazing opportunities.

But take a moment to consider whether always taking the easy option and going along the same familiar path is helping you experience the full richness of life.

You see, sometimes success, fulfilment, and happiness may be lurking just a short distance outside your comfort zone.

Do you have the courage to discover them?

The good news is you can have your cake and eat it. But you've got to take action before you can enjoy it.

And you've got to overcome the curse of comfort.

Chapter 33

FLEX FOR SUCCESS

The son of a vicar from Shrewsbury is often credited with words he actually didn't say.

They go something like this:

> The future does not belong to the strongest or the most intelligent. The future belongs to those who are best able to adapt to change.

The vicar's son was Charles Darwin.

Whoever did say it certainly hit on a truth, though, didn't they?

It's not always about how successful you've been, it's how successful you are currently that counts. Many an organization can boast of a glorious past: Kodak, Blockbuster, Woolworths. But it's their failure to adapt to change that led to their demise.

In our own lives we can also be hindered by our lack of flexibility or willingness to adapt to the world around us.

Great Life Insight

It's easy to cling on to our current ways of doing things and to justify our stubborn refusal to change as a strength.

But sometimes we need to stop, reflect, and ask ourselves how our existing approach to life is working for us.

Is it helping us or hindering us?

Is our stubbornness a strength born out of a sense of drive, determination, and focus, or a weakness born out of a fear of change and a desire to cling to the past? Only you can answer that question honestly. But here's something worth considering:

Great Life Insight

Just because a path is well trodden doesn't mean it's the best way to go.

Perhaps by being more flexible and less rigid in how we do life we'll actually achieve greater success and happiness.

That's certainly advice I've needed to take myself. Let me explain.

I'm probably best known for two things. To my family I'm known for having the worst sense of direction in the entire history of humanity. They even joke I need help finding my way out of an elevator.

However, to those outside my family, I'm probably best known for the phrase SUMO – Shut Up, Move On. It's the title of my biggest-selling book and also my brand. I'm known as the SUMO guy.

But let me share how I've needed to flex for success and adapt my approach in terms of my business.

Several years ago, I wanted to develop my material and make it accessible for children in schools. I hired a primary school teacher, a secondary school teacher, and a youth worker to help me do so. And thus, SUMO4Schools was born.

The SUMO approach was adopted by a number of schools. However, I had a rather interesting and ultimately game-changing conversation with the headteacher of a primary school. It went something like this:

'Paul, I'm a big fan. I love your SUMO book. So does my husband, and he rarely reads books. My staff loved the training you did with them, and I'm delighted to say the children are really enjoying the SUMO lessons too.'

But I sensed there was a three-letter word looming on the not too distant horizon.

And I wasn't wrong.

'But ... I still don't like what SUMO stands for. I know "Shut Up" isn't meant to be aggressive. I know what you really mean by those words, but I have a problem.'

'OK, go on Diane, I'm all ears.'

'Well, I had a parent ask me recently what SUMO was. Her son George had been doing some SUMO activities in his class and she was intrigued to know more. The problem is, Paul, I felt really uncomfortable saying it stands for Shut Up, Move On. George is seven. We actually tell our children in the school that it's disrespectful to use the phrase "Shut up."'

'So, here's what I'd like you to do. Change the title. Because if you're not able to, much as it pains me, I really don't think I'd feel comfortable continuing to use the programme with the children.'

As I listened I have to confess that my first response was to defend my corner.

'But Diane, it's my brand. It's what I'm known for. It's taken me years to develop', I replied.

'I understand that Paul. And like I said, I love your work, but unless you change the title I don't think we'll be able to use it anymore.'

So, what did I do?

Well, let's just take a moment to revisit that earlier quote:

> The future does not belong to the strongest or the most intelligent. The future belongs to those who are best able to adapt to change.

It seemed rather pertinent for me at that moment.

There are several thousand primary schools in the UK. That's a huge number of young people SUMO could help. And I began wondering if it was only Diane who had a problem with the words 'Shut Up'.

If I was honest I thought not.

But if McDonald's can sell salads (which they have been doing since 2005) then maybe I could be more flexible in my approach.

It took me a few weeks but with the input of my team we came up with a way forward. SUMO does still stand for Shut Up, Move On, but it can now also stand for this:

Stop, Understand, Move On.

And Diane's school is still happy to use SUMO.

Now I'm not suggesting we abandon our principles or don't remain true to our values. Far from it. I'm simply saying we need to be adaptable. In fact, with new technology rapidly changing the way we live and work, I believe it's crucial we adapt. The reality is that no matter how successful we've been in the past, it's what we do now that counts.

Great Life Insight

The species that survive are those that adapt to their environment, not those that fight it.

So, a great life comes from being open to ideas, having a willingness to adapt, and an awareness that what worked in the past might not work so well now.

It's about dealing with the world as it is, not as you want it to be.

As a motivational speaker from Manchester once said,

> Stubbornness is a choice – it's not a medical condition.

And that's why, to have a great life, we need to flex for success.

Chapter 34

SHOW SOME LEADERSHIP

I love to tweet about all kinds of subjects (you can connect @TheSumoGuy). Two of my most popular tweets were in relation to the time I failed to comment on my wife's new jumper, and when I didn't notice that she'd had her hair cut. My lack of observational skills was duly noted.

Those tweets were sent from my hospital bed.

But even they failed to get the level of engagement of this one:

Great Life Insight

The older I get, the more I realize this: there are too many people called leaders, but not enough leadership.

Now your first response might be to agree with the statement but not see it as relevant to you, as you're not a leader.

Well I've got news for you: you are.

It might not be your title, but showing leadership is crucial if you want to get the most from life. Here's why.

When you research 'traits of a leader' you discover answers such as showing initiative, taking responsibility, courage, influence, setting an example, being flexible, and taking positive action. Well, in my book these are all traits that will enhance anyone's life. Admittedly we might not lead others, but here's the deal – we all need to lead ourselves.

I recognize none of us are actually born as leaders. When we're born we're more dependent on others for our survival than almost any other species.

But we do grow up, at least physically anyway, and as we do so, barring any health or medical issues, become less dependent on others. (I recognize parents of some teenagers may strongly contest that fact, however.)

But not everyone grows up emotionally, and perhaps one of the clearest signs of this is when we fail to take responsibility for our actions, and behave like powerless people expecting others to fulfill and meet our needs.

Now of course we need the support of others. But we also need to grow up and mature into people who recognize we have responsibility for our own actions and decisions.

The key to doing this is to start by reflecting on how we see ourselves. Our self-perception is crucial.

For example, if we see ourselves as having little influence, control, or power in how our lives develop, then we're likely to live a passive, reactive, and fatalistic life. We can have hopes and dreams, but ultimately whether they become a reality is in the hands of fate, luck, or perhaps a divine being.

But if you see yourself as a leader who is able to shape and influence your future, the outcome is very different.

Here's the deal:

Whatever you think and feel about yourself and your life will ultimately impact how you live your life. If I were you, I'd re-read that sentence. It's powerful stuff.

Great Life Insight

The story you tell yourself about who you are and why you're here will shape your behaviour and your future.

So, in a nutshell, a change in identity can lead to a change of behaviour. Not convinced? Well, here's an example to illustrate my point.

Occasionally I am invited by a friend to watch Manchester United.

He has rather nice seats, too. And it's a privilege to go.

But here's my point. I don't support Manchester United. However, when I go I behave like a United fan (I always have prawn sandwiches at half time). If I didn't, I'd never be invited back again. If United concede a goal (which I admit is a remote possibility if they're playing Bradford or Wigan) I don't stand and cheer – I value my safety too much.

You see, my temporary identity influences how I behave.

Here's another way of thinking about it.

Imagine if what you thought about yourself was encapsulated in a word or short phrase and was printed on a T-shirt you wore every day. Now, depending on the message on your T-shirt, that could actually feel quite empowering. Just as wearing the shirt of your favourite sports team identifies who you are, so too would the message on your T-shirt.

However, perhaps the real power of the message is not what it sends out to others but, more importantly, what message you're telling yourself.

You see, whatever that message is, whatever story we're telling ourselves, really does influence how we behave.

So, let me ask you a question, to which only honest answers are allowed.

If there was a message on your T-shirt, what would it say?

Because if that message isn't a positive or empowering one, I suggest it's time to invest in a new wardrobe.

One of the biggest lessons I've learnt from over 50 years on the planet is this:

Great Life Insight

If you want a great life, quit waiting for it to happen. It's up to you to do something.

Pray, if that's part of your beliefs, but recognize you could very well be the answer to your own prayers.

Great Life Tip

Start looking within yourself for some answers rather than waiting for someone else to rescue you.

We might have been born helpless, but we don't have to remain that way.

You're not a passive bystander watching your life unfold. You're in the game. You're the driver, not some reluctant passenger.

Life is happening now. So, it's time to wake up and not doze through our days.

It's time to face up to our responsibilities and to do all within our power (however limited that may be) to be the best version of ourselves we can be and to also do what we can to help others.

You may never lead a team, a business, or an organization, but that doesn't stop you showing some leadership and making a positive difference.

I'm challenged by these words from Barack Obama. I hope you are too:

> Change will not come if we wait for some other person or some other time. We are the ones we've been waiting for. We are the change that we seek.

That's so powerful, don't you think? I reckon I'll have to tweet that.

Chapter 35

TAKE YOUR TALK FOR A WALK

There's a condition I think many people in modern society suffer from. I call it 'Action Illusion'.

Symptoms include always appearing busy, continually complaining about a lack of time, and spending endless hours in meetings. Of all the symptoms that can lead to the condition becoming chronic, talking about what you're going to do as opposed to actually doing anything about it is the most common.

Great Life Insight

Action Illusion causes people to confuse activity with effectiveness; to believe being busy means we're being productive.

Now I understand why people can be seduced by the appeal of busyness. It can make us feel important. And it's easy to confuse motion and movement with actual progress.

Let me explain what I mean by that.

A toy rocking horse creates a lot of motion, but it doesn't get anywhere does it? And endless conversations about what you're going to do are not a substitute for actually doing something.

Agreed?

By the way, I love that rocking horse illustration, don't you?

You see, a great life is not created by simply talking about it. Having endless meetings and lots of planning can become a rather subtle but also dangerous way of avoiding a decision or taking any action.

Here's the deal: long hours and working harder are not the keys to your success.

Great Life Insight

It's not the hours you put in, it's what you put into your hours that counts.

Yes, it's important to talk and plan, but it needs to lead to something: action.

For instance, reading this book is an activity. It takes up your time. I would love it if you talked about it with friends. But your life doesn't become great due to what you read, or who you discuss it with. That may help, but ultimately it becomes great because of how it causes you to act.

So, what stops us taking action?

I believe there are lots of factors, but here's one I think is both subtle and deceptive – it's when we become a slave to our emotions.

In other words, we're waiting for the right feelings before we do anything.

We're waiting to feel motivated, confident, or creative before we start something.

The problem is, if you're waiting for the right feelings before you take action, you could be waiting a long time.

I genuinely believe the key to much of what we need to do in life is not that complicated. But we make it complicated, by overanalysing and overthinking our every decision and allowing our emotions to become obstacles to our actions.

So, how do you overcome this?

First, start with the following:

Great Life Tip

Be clear on what you want to do and, crucially, why you want to do it.

Here are three questions to help with this:

- 'What's the one thing I absolutely have to do today?'

- 'What's the very first action I need to take to do this?'

- 'What are the consequences if I don't do it?'

And in order to avoid confusing activity with effectiveness, here's another question to ask:

- 'Is what I'm doing now taking me closer to my goal?' (If not, why are you doing it?)

Once you've answered these questions, start taking action.

Here's another quote from the motivational speaker Zig Ziglar:

You don't have to be great to start, but you do have to start to be great.

He's got a point.

I'm writing this book in the midst of an incredibly busy speaking schedule, but the key to writing it is to start writing it. Simple, eh? And it's more likely to happen when you realize this:

Great Life Insight

It's your daily decisions and disciplines that determine your success rather than how you're feeling that day.

And if you want to know what separates successful people from the rest of the crowd, commit this next sentence to memory:

Commitment is the ability to carry on long after the excitement has gone.

I rarely get excited about taking exercise (in fact, I'm never excited) but I'm committed to doing it. I don't talk about it, or spend endless hours working out an exercise routine and what gear to wear.

I do it.

It's based on a decision, not a feeling.

So, let me be blunt with you.

Your great life won't happen because you dream about it. And much as we'd like it to, the universe isn't going to serve it up to you on a plate.

You've got to do something.

You've got to take your talk for a walk and maybe today would be a good day to start.

Because if you don't ... well, how about you reflect on these words of Steve Jobs:

Great Life Challenge

'One day you will wake up and there won't be any more time to do the things you've always wanted. Do it now.'

A life of success, fulfilment, and happiness does not just happen by accident.

It happens by action.

So, quit the talking and do some walking.

Today.

Now it's Over to You

In the introduction to this book I wrote that we were embarking on a journey together. Well, the journey is coming to an end (at least for the moment, anyway). Over the last 35 chapters we've explored ideas and insights that could help us to have a great life by increasing our levels of success, fulfilment, and happiness. Each of those three areas is subjective and not easy to measure. However, I do hope you feel it's been a worthwhile ride. I genuinely hope that you have gained not only some insights and ideas, but crucially also some inspiration to help you make a difference during your time on this planet.

The reality is, over a hundred billion people have lived on this planet before you, but there's never been a single person just like you. And there never will be. You are unique. So, my question is, how will you maximize this incredible privilege and this amazing opportunity called life? How can you make a difference not just to yourself, but also to others?

Life provides endless possibilities, and each of us has so much potential. The challenge is to recognize we cannot do life in isolation, but to understand that our effectiveness and enjoyment are increased significantly when we connect and collaborate with others.

It starts by not taking miracles for granted. So, wake up to the fact that this is your time, your opportunity. Your life isn't a rehearsal – it's the main show. It will pass really quickly if you don't take time to savour and enjoy it. I love this quote attributed to Confucius: 'We all have two lives. The second one starts when we realize we only have one.'

The last idea I shared with you was 'Take your talk for a walk.' So, although I wish a great life could be achieved simply by reading or listening to a book, the reality is somewhat different. So, I've some advice, and also a couple of favours to ask.

Firstly, take time in the next few months to re-read this book. You'll be surprised what you notice from reading it a second time that you didn't see before. Although the content won't have changed, you and your circumstances will have. So, I strongly encourage you to see this as a book you return to time and time again.

If you haven't already done so, take notes, highlight certain phrases, and identify small, simple actions you can take (remember, molehills matter massively).

As I also mentioned in my introduction, share your ideas from reading this book with others. Not only could you be helping them, but you'll be helping yourself cement your learning and understanding.

And now for those favours. If you've benefited from reading this book, tweet some of your favourite quotes to @TheSumoGuy (use #greatlife). It's really helpful to hear what's resonated with you.

Secondly, I'm very keen to know which chapters in particular helped you. So, I would love you to email Paul. McGee@theSUMOguy.com with your top three chapters. Who knows, your feedback might encourage me to write a follow-up with further ideas on how to have a great life.

I've shared many quotes in this book, so let me leave you with one of my favourites. It's from Ralph Waldo Emerson.

> To laugh often and much, to win the respect of intelligent people and the affection of children ... to leave the world a bit better ... to know even one life has breathed easier because you lived. This is to have succeeded.

That's all from me. The ball is now in your court. It's time to make your mark. To make a difference. So, over to you.

Thanks for sharing the journey. And here's to a great life.

Paul
2018

With Special Thanks To . . .

I'm hugely grateful and privileged to know and work with some incredible people. Those that helped specifically with this book are Kev Daniels, Sally Blackburn-Daniels, Ed and Sarah Hollamby, Matt Summerfield, and Catriona Hudson. Guys, your support has been invaluable. Thank you.

My wife Helen has also proved both insightful and encouraging with her feedback, and I'm so thankful that my daughter Ruth (known to me as Ruffio) patiently listened to me read out extracts from the book. So glad you like it. My son Matt has wisdom beyond his years, and I'm grateful for his perspective and thoughts that influence my thinking more than he will ever know.

With gratitude.

About Paul McGee

Paul McGee is a conference speaker, seminar presenter, communication coach, and bestselling author.

His academic background is in behavioural and social psychology, and his early career was spent in Human Resources and People Development.

He's one of the UK's leading speakers on change, inspiring leadership, and communicating with confidence. His thought-provoking, humorous, and practical approach to life has seen him speak in 41 countries and he's sold over 200,000 books worldwide. He also works on a consultancy and coaching basis with an English Premier League football team.

He developed the SUMO (Shut Up, Move On) brand in 2002 and more recently launched SUMO4Schools, a programme designed to help young people realize their potential and develop skills for life.

He's fascinated by people, an explorer of faith, and passionate about football. He supports two teams – Wigan Athletic and Bradford City. Why? It's a long story.

Good food and laughter with family and friends, coupled with walks in the countryside, keep him sane. Most of the time.

To find out more about his work visit www.theSUMOguy .com

Other Books by Paul McGee

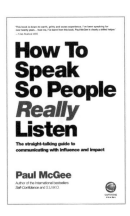

How To Speak So People Really Listen: The straight-talking guide to communicating with influence and impact (2017)

How to Succeed With People: Remarkably Easy Ways to Engage, Influence and Motivate Almost Anyone (2013)

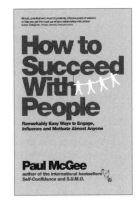

S.U.M.O. (Shut Up, Move On), 10th Anniversary Edition: The Straight-Talking Guide to Succeeding in Life (2015)

How Not to Worry: The Remarkable Truth of How A Small Change Can Help You Stress Less and Enjoy Life More (2012)

Self-Confidence, Second Edition: The Remarkable Truth of Why A Small Change Can Make a Big Difference (2012)

S.U.M.O. Your Relationships: How to Handle Not Strangle The People You Live and Work With (2007)

Want Paul to Speak for Your Organization?

Paul McGee speaks around the world at conferences and company events. From a keynote address to half- and full-day seminars, Paul tailors his message according to your requirements. His goal is to provide insights, inspiration, and practical tools people can use immediately, in both their professional and personal lives, and to communicate his message in an entertaining and highly engaging way.

For more details on how Paul or one of his team can help your organization, contact us via:

Telephone: +44 (0)1925 268708

Email: Paul.McGee@theSUMOguy.com

Web: www.theSUMOguy.com

Index